WHAT OUR

Friends

LEFT BEHIND

Grief and *Laughter*
in a Pandemic

Victoria Noe

Edited by Jay Blotcher
Cover and Interior Design by 100 Covers

ISBN 979-8988240501 (hardcover)
ISBN 979-8988240518 (paperback)
ISBN 979-8988240525 (ebook)
ISBN 979-8988240532 (audiobook)

First edition: September, 2023

This project is partially supported by a grant from the Illinois Arts Council Agency.

King Company Publishing
4231 N. Springfield Ave.
Chicago, IL 60618
www.victorianoe.com

To the friends I have grieved during this pandemic: Mrs. Balloni, Mr. D'Angelo, Mrs. Adams, Bradley, Richard, Raymond, Christy, Tim, Kathy, Sharon, Hunter, Rebecca, Mel, Mrs. Guthrie, Andy, Steve.

And to the friends you have lost during this challenging time.

This book is for them.

And for you.

Contents

friendship
is
romance

i want a world where friendship is appreciated as a form of romance. i want a
world where when people ask if we are seeing anyone we can list the names of all
of our best friends and no one will bat an eyelid. i want monuments and holidays
and certificates and ceremonies to commemorate friendship. i want a world that
doesn't require us to be in a sexual/romantic partnership to be seen as mature (let
alone complete). i want a movement that fights for all forms of relationships, not
just the sexual ones. i want thousands of songs and movies and poems about the
intimacy between friends. i want a world where our worth isn't linked to our
desireability, our security to our monogamy, our family to our biology.[1]

Never forget Nerinx or me either.
—Christy Adams[1]

When I first got the idea for this book, I assumed I would lose a friend during COVID; maybe more than one. I hoped it would not approach the number of friends lost during the dark early days of AIDS, but in March of 2020, that was not assured. It was surprising that almost a full year passed before any friends died.

But I guess my luck ran out because by the end of 2022, there were a dozen more on the list. In February of 2022,

I gave my first eulogy for one of my oldest and dearest friends. It was a miserably cold, icy day in St. Louis when we said goodbye to Christy Adams.

Author, Sue Lunnemann, Lynn McSorley, Christy Adams,
Nerinx Hall parking lot, May, 1970,
permission of Lynn McSorley

Christy and I met freshman year at Nerinx Hall, a Catholic girls high school in Webster Groves, a suburb of St. Louis. Run by the Sisters of Loretto, it was and is described as 'dangerously liberal'. Our high school years coincided with the height of the civil rights movement and the Vietnam War. Christy and I marked the first Earth Day senior year, and graduated a few weeks after the May 1970 Kent

State killings. Christy had an ingrained fashion sense, no doubt passed on by her elegant mother, and a passion for theater that rivaled my own.

She was loyal and dependable and genuine, and she never missed sending a card on birthdays, anniversaries, or Christmas. Until 2020. That's how I realized something was going on that she wasn't telling me. She had been diagnosed with cancer.

Of all the friends I've ever known, Christy was among the most private. She had a very clear sense of what personal information she was willing to share, even as she expected you to be much more forthcoming. When she and our friend Lynn and I had lunch in July of 2021, everything seemed fine. Her cancer appeared to be in the past, or at least at a manageable stage, as I don't remember it being part of our conversation. She looked great, perfectly put together as always, but mentioned an unusual pain that she'd have to tell her doctor about. When things began to go downhill a couple months later, our periodic phone calls grew more serious. She told me more about what she was going through than I ever imagined she would. In fact, she volunteered information that I would never have asked for, knowing her penchant for privacy. And though I was surprised, I knew that her trust in me was something to cherish.

Christy and her mother both had COVID in 2020. But in the fall of 2021, COVID restrictions on visiting patients in hospitals and rehabilitation centers were still in place. I sent her cards and called; she didn't seem to have the strength to email. More than once my husband asked if I wanted to drive down to St. Louis to visit her. But my answer was always the same: "I can't. Only her sister and one of her brothers can visit her." Near the end, I offered to come down if she wanted to see me, but I knew that was unlikely. Christy was very particular about her appearance, and even though we'd been friends for well over 50 years, I knew she would not have wanted me to see her like that.

Though I understood, and agreed that it was her right to restrict visitors, it added to the helplessness I felt. I wanted to do something, anything, that might lift her mood.

That's when I remembered my friend Delle Chatman. She'd fought ovarian cancer for four years, going into remission for a while and then experiencing a return. When the cancer reappeared, she decided after a month to discontinue treatment, announcing her decision in an email to friends.

The reaction was swift, with most vocalizing their dismay. She'd beaten back the cancer before -- more than once.

She could do it again, right? But Delle recognized that her body was simply too weak to keep fighting. Her decision was not up for debate: she was at peace, even if her friends were not. So we responded again, this time expressing the love and admiration we had for her. Delle was not amused. "I'm not dead yet! Save it for the funeral; I'll be there."

I never asked if she was embarrassed by the show of affection or whether she felt disturbed reading these eulogies. I imagine it was a little of both. But one thing was true: she died in November 2006, knowing just how loved she was by so many. And I wanted the same for Christy.

So Lynn and I decided to campaign Christy and her sister for the right to share her health news -- she was now receiving hospice care -- with our Nerinx Hall class. Not a public announcement on Facebook, but an email only to our classmates. We didn't want to be pushy, but I was beginning to feel the weight of keeping this secret from our friends. It was a weight that was not just emotional, but felt physical, as well. She did agree, and we sent out an email to the class.

What happened next was similar to what happened with Delle. But whereas Delle had been able to have visitors in her condo up to the end, our class could only send cards. And boy, did they. During our reunion weekend in June of 2022, Christy's sister Mary Ellen joined us at one event to thank us for the show of love. "It was like Christmas!" she marveled, recounting how every day multiple cards arrived in the mail. It meant a lot to Christy and her family. And it lifted a little of that burden of helplessness I felt. She died in February 2022.

COVID -- but not only COVID -- limited access to Christy's funeral. On that dreary winter day, numerous ice storms passed through the St. Louis area, a municipality not known for stellar snow removal. The roads were dangerous, and that -- as much as COVID -- kept most of Christy's friends home. Only three of us from our class made it to the church. There were maybe fifteen people in the pews who were not family. None of her classmates made it to the funeral parlor or cemetery

The tiny crowd made me sad and angry: Christy deserved a church full of friends who loved her. But at least the service was live-streamed, thanks to a request from classmate Carol Greco. The church agreed to do so because of the extreme weather, so classmates from as far away as Quebec could watch.

Two days after Christy died on February 19, 2022, I was packing to drive down to St. Louis for the funeral. Just then, I got a text from Christy's sister: "The family would be honored if you would give the eulogy." My first thought was, "Oh, hell, no!" I was going to have a hard enough time getting through the funeral. But after debating myself for a while, I agreed. I had about 48 hours to prepare.

I'd never given a eulogy before, so my only experience was hearing eulogies for family and friends. Should I be serious and respectful? Is there room for humor? How could I possibly do justice to a woman who was so loved?

I reached out to the class. Did anyone have a story about Christy they wanted to share? I wanted it to be a group project, because the grief was not only mine. I got enough stories to get started, and spent most of those two days in my room at the Holiday Inn at Watson & Lindbergh writing and rewriting. Rehearsing in front of a mirror to make sure I didn't talk too fast but stayed within the time limit.

I was already stressed when I reached the church, after driving through the first ice storm. I got under control – until the procession began and the casket was wheeled up the aisle. For an instant, I flashed back to the first funeral I ever attended for a friend: the brother of one of my girlfriends, killed the first week he was in Vietnam, in the summer of 1968.

The procession had stopped and the casket was next to me. I caught my breath, both times, and now wondered if I could get through the next hour. When I was rehearsing the eulogy in my hotel room, I noted that I could get through the whole thing before my voice cracked at one particular line near the end. But here I was, before Mass even started, struggling. So I took a deep breath and wiped the tears that seeped under my KF94 mask.

We've all been to too many funerals where the minister didn't know the person who died. So the best part of Christy's funeral was that the priest was a friend of hers. I'd heard her talk about Billy Huette many times over the years; they'd met at Spring Hill College. He and I chatted briefly before Mass, but did not discuss what we were going to say. I was pleasantly surprised by his beautiful sermon about their friendship. It was the perfect lead-in to my eulogy.

I earned two degrees in theater, so I have no fear of getting up in front of an audience. I also know how to use a microphone, which would be important for the live streaming. I was not intimidated walking up to the lectern. I looked out at the family, took a deep breath to center myself, and began to speak:

Thank you to Father Huette and to the entire Adams family for granting me the honor of speaking today representing the Nerinx Hall class of 1970. I hesitated to do it, but I was pretty sure Christy would be annoyed if I didn't.

But all my rehearsal time turned out to be wasted. My voice cracked on the first sentence.

That was not a good sign: my eulogy was going to run five minutes. I took another deep breath and kept talking, careful not to talk too fast. I was sure to include humor, because being friends with Christy always meant a lot of laughter. One of her cousins, who sat right in my line of vision, laughed more than anyone, which gave me the confidence to go on:

> When the news went out to our class, several girls reached out to me. Judie Hennies, Kathy Cunningham, Ann Finney, Kathy Mosher, all expressing their grief over the loss of this wonderful friend.
>
> I remember a day in the fall of 1966 in Speech class when Mrs. Des Parois -- for some reason -- decided we should demonstrate how we answer the phone at home. So, using a prop telephone, we each took a turn saying 'Hello.' Then Christy's turn came:

"Adams residence, Christy speaking." Even Mrs. Des Parois was impressed.

Christy and I passed notes in school -- yes, we did -- and wrote many letters to each other. Before she left for Spring Hill College, she wrote that she had heard that people stay closer to their college friends than their high school friends. And she hoped that didn't happen to us. When I visited her there over spring break freshman year, I was glad she had new friends, but didn't let go of old ones.

Christy was a human Google. She knew everybody, maybe not personally, but she knew about them. At first, I assumed she knew so much because of meeting people at her mother's shop. But it wasn't just that. She soaked up information and stored it away. Anytime I asked, "I wonder what so-and-so is doing?" she would have a detailed answer at the ready.

In the fall of 1972, she wrote to me from Spring Hill with the following St. Louis news:

"I had a letter from Lynn yesterday. Kane's getting married May 19. Patty Van Wie will be matron of honor.

*She's supposed to get married March 17. Don't you go
and get married, too, or I'll murder you."*

A few years later, she wrote from grad school in
Quebec City, full of news about people in St. Louis.
I remember staring at the letter and thinking, "I'm
here and I don't know any of this. How did you find
out?" I should've known by then not to question.

It wasn't gossip. That has a negative connotation,
suggesting things that are made up or malicious.
And while the stories she told could be a little
snarky, they were never malicious. There was the
occasional raised eyebrow, but otherwise she simply reported the facts. Her sources were impecca-
ble. I always got excited -- as I did not too long ago --
whenever I could tell her, "I have some really
good gossip."

Earlier this month I was in New York City. I bought
a card at the Cooper Hewitt Museum to send her
because I had a lot to share: mostly my reviews of
Hadestown and *Company,* but also a couple of great
backstage stories from a Broadway actor I interviewed for my next book. The day after that interview, Lynn called to tell me that Christy had taken
a turn for the worst.

So I sent her some chocolate and a different card with a different sentiment: telling her that she has always been my kindest and most loyal friend, and for that I'll always be grateful.

Our 50th high school reunion is coming up at the beginning of June, delayed twice because of COVID. Carol Greco reminded me that Christy worked on every one of our reunions. I always enjoyed the follow-up almost as much as the reunions themselves because Christy and I would compare notes: Who did you talk to? What did you find out?

The last time I talked to Christy was the middle of January. She was, as she had been on our calls for several months, really down. I listened to her frustrations but I couldn't think of much to say that would ease them. Instead I blurted out, "Listen, I don't want to go to the reunion without you." And she said, "Well, I don't want you to go without me."

I still don't want to.

Christy was simply the best of us. She was a Nerinx girl who gave of herself every day: in her work, in the way she treated those around her, in her faith.

Of course, I know she would not want us to be sad. She would want us to pull together, which we are doing here today. And to tell the people we love that we love them. Not just family, but friends, too.

I hope that I was half as good a friend to Christy as she was to me. Because she always was and always will be an inspiration to me. We were all lucky to know her.

In our senior yearbook, she wrote: *Never forget Nerinx or me either.*

I promise I won't."[2]

When I got to the part where my voice had always cracked while rehearsing, this time it did not crack. This time I struggled to stay in control. I was determined to get through it, and I did. I walked back to my pew, pausing to touch her casket. And then I stopped holding back the tears.

Our 50th class reunion was delayed twice because of COVID. The first year we knew it was impossible to get together. We channeled our disappointment into fulfilling a request made by Carol Greco: For our class to write letters of support to the graduating seniors, whose prom and graduation were canceled. The second year postpone-ment was more of a disappointment, because things had started to open up. But Nerinx was not hosting big events yet. And given the fragile health of some classmates, we delayed again to 2022. Our reunion finally happened less than four months after Christy's funeral. She had told her oncologist that all she wanted was to make it to the re-union. The COVID delays stole that dream from her.

Chrstine Adams, Sea Island, undated photo,
with permission of Adams family

For a while I was on the fence about going to the Nerinx re-union, because I kept remembering my last conversation with Christy, when I said I didn't want to go without her. I still didn't want to, but I did. The tears were much few-er than I'd feared because I was surrounded by Christy's friends. In fact, I got through almost the whole weekend without crying. But it was at the last event, a Sunday morning prayer service, that the tears finally came.

We graduated 113 girls in 1970; there are 95 left. Our reunion tradition is to remember those who have died by reciting their names and presenting a rose at the front of the altar/podium during the service. The roses were brought up in order, beginning with one for the classmate who died while we were still in high school. That meant Christy was last. I was not surprised to be asked to bring up her rose, and I didn't feel sad about it. But when I sat back down, my friend Judie grabbed my hand. And that did it. I began crying more than I had since the funeral, and it took me a few minutes to regain control.

I've grieved in groups before, with friends and family. That's the normal ritual that we were denied during COVID: the ability to share grief and love in person. For the first time since before the pandemic, I felt a palpable relief to be able to grieve with others, even more so than at Christy's funeral. And I thanked God yet again that she didn't die a year earlier, in February 2021 like her mother did, when gathering was still impossible. I spent the weekend laughing more than crying, which was my goal. I was surrounded by classmates who looked the same and different, who acted the same and different. That familiarity was a comfort I needed, even if I still wasn't friends with all of them. That's okay. We're long past the need to impress each other.

Christy is not my only friend who died during COVID, and not even the most recent one. As I write this, sixteen friends have died during the pandemic, although only one of them from the virus. As always, some losses were expected, some were not. I was only able to attend one other service besides Christy's, also in 2022, because of attendance restrictions or lack of live streaming. Some were delayed until gathering in person was safer. One death I didn't find out until weeks after the funeral because his husband isn't on social media.

I was lucky to be able to grieve Christy and Sharon in person. But that leaves a lot of solitary grieving for me, and my experience is far from unique. COVID has upended the way we grieve. And at a time when draconian limits were placed on family members, the friends left behind found themselves even more restricted from comforting and grieving as they normally would. In the book *Alone Together*, Laura Stanfill shared the story of losing her dear friend of thirty years, Priya. Her experience was typical:

The news comes from her sister like all the other updates these past two weeks: by text. A friend reports it's appropriate to wear white to Priya's funeral, so Justin, Melissa, and I hunt in our closets. I find a gauzy scarf with bronze embroidered flowers, pair it with a white and gray paisley dress with hints of gold. I go to my parents' house to attend the funeral. Our cameras are off; we are all on mute. The priest sings prayers. The family sprinkles Priya's white casket with petals and spices. The funeral home workers wheel her away. One isn't wearing a mask. The family follows the body, singing prayers and wailing. We keep watch over the empty room until someone thinks to turn us off.[3]

There was a brief moment, as I prepared to write Christy's eulogy, when I toyed with the idea of quoting the minister in the film *The Big Chill*: "I'm angry, and I don't know what to do with my anger." Anger may be the last taboo when it comes to grief, and there has been plenty of it during COVID. For many people, it was a shock to feel an emotion that's not considered acceptable. But looking back on all of this, why wouldn't we be angry?

This is not a self-help book or a substitute for therapy. It's not a political statement on the pandemic, though politics are referred to occasionally, because, let's face it, it can't be helped.

This book is not an instructional manual on how to do grief. Anyone trying to sell one of those is scamming you because grief can't be taught any more than it can be avoided or fixed. It can only be lived, in all its devastating, enraging, world-altering ways.

Instead, this book is for those of us who still struggle with ways to grieve and honor the friends who died these past three years during the COVID pandemic. It's an attempt at solidarity, to assure you that you are not alone in your grief.

With every true friendship,
we build more firmly the foundations
on which the peace of the whole world rests.[1]

Over one million dead, just in the U.S.

It's often reported that every death leaves behind an average of nine people who mourn that person. Friends are rarely included in the calculation of death's impact. We know that because workplace bereavement policies -- including the Family and Medical Leave Act -- make no provisions for friends. But with over one million dead from COVID -- and about 300,000 more considered 'excess deaths' -- that's a lot of grieving friends. A 13-year study of over 26,000 Australians found that the grief over the death of a close friend can last four years or more. And that was before COVID.

What does that estimate of losing 1 million people mean? According to a study by the University of Arkansas for Medical Sciences (UAMS) Office of Community Health and Research, one-quarter of all adults in the US have lost a family member or friend to this pandemic.

> "COVID-19 robbed us of our goodbyes," says Dr. Joy Miller of Peoria, Illinois. "My friend was suddenly gone without warning. How do I say goodbye? I can't travel. We aren't allowed to gather, and I will never see him again. I don't know what to do. I feel lost and empty, as if my heart is being ripped from my body."[2]

Few people I interviewed could describe their daily interactions without mentioning the role of friends. Our friends are our neighbors, classmates, coworkers, people we volunteer with. With varying degrees of closeness, they're people we grew up with, and increasingly they are people we only know online. We met them when our kids went to school together, and for the lucky few, those friendships lasted long after graduation. Families are important, no question, and easier to define. When we struggle to define friendships important to us, we often fall back on calling people a "best friend" or say "they're like family to me."

That's not a new challenge, because calling someone a friend often feels like an inadequate way to define a relationship that means the world to us.

Our brains are hardwired for social interaction. What happens when that intimate connection is restricted to online meetings due to a frightening new virus?

Lydia Denworth, author of the book *Friendship*, knows exactly what happens: "Friendship is not just cultural. It changes our health, our biology, and the trajectory of our lives." Social interaction is crucial to our health, including boosting our immune systems. "Friendship is as important as diet and exercise for your health. Even more important on some levels." Loneliness was identified as a public health concern long before COVID.

That said, many took the pandemic as an opportunity for reflection on all parts of life, including friendships. Kat Vellos, author of *We Should Get Together: The Secret to Cultivating Better Friendships*, discussed that kind of reflection:

"Being forced apart made us realize which bonds and whose closeness we craved the most, and whose we were OK going without. Many people realized that some of their former friendships were just based on convenience or habit, and that they lacked deputy or true commitment."[3]

One experience that played out throughout the pandemic was the realization that we had friends who did not share our values. Whether it was the lockdown restrictions, mask mandates, or vaccines, a polarization arose in our society that made it difficult to maintain certain relationships. It's up to every individual to decide what continuing a friendship is worth, because as Vellos points out,

"The four seeds of connection are proximity, frequency, commitment, and compatibility...Having all four makes things easier, but you don't need them all to be at 100 percent to still have a healthy friendship."[4]

The pandemic's negative effect on relationships - intensified by election-year passions - is one of its defining aspects. For some people, it was a never-before-seen rage, often directed at specific demographic groups. For others, it was the casual dismissal of at-risk populations, and the realization that you were in a demographic that people you loved were suddenly willing to sacrifice for their own convenience. If that felt like a betrayal of friendship, that's understandable. Why remain friends with someone who felt your life was disposable?

The pandemic also shone a spotlight on class differences. Families that moved out of big cities like New York, retreating to smaller communities that they deemed safe, left behind friends who did not have that option. Jobs designated as essential were often those held by people of color and the poor, keeping them at work and putting them at much greater risk of contracting the coronavirus.

Social media was both a blessing and a curse, especially in the early days of COVID. The challenges thrown at various industries were profound, as were those experienced by each of us trying to access services and products. For anyone without reliable internet access, much less a home office, the inability to obtain information and medical assistance became a matter of life or death. Libraries, long a lifeline for those without their own computers, were closed. Loneliness soared.

Still, for those lucky enough to have internet service, having lots of friends on social media doesn't always mean those friendships are deep and meaningful. During COVID, it likely meant only that they were the ones it was easier to keep in touch with. A disproportionate number may have been coworkers. But if your closest friends don't use social media, what does that mean for those friendships in a time of social isolation? It means we kept in touch via tried-and-true methods, including telephone or snail mail.

What of the friends you're not that close to? I don't suggest that your friendship has unraveled, or you no longer have as much in common. I refer to those outer circles of friendship that we take for granted: the people we interact with on a regular basis, and whose names we may not know. Like New Yorkers after 9/11, people across the country felt the loss of community that exists with circles of friends. These circles included not only your coworkers or neighbors, the friends you are physically closest to every day. They also include widening circles: the bodega clerk who sells you a bacon, egg and cheese bagel every morning. The people who share your commute on the same train every morning. The barista who starts making your "usual" as soon as you walk in the door. The bus driver who asks about your kids. The people who work out at the gym the same time you do.

One day they're there; the next day they're gone.

After 9/11, too, the loss of these casual social interactions added to the grief of losing coworkers when the towers fell. You may consider them to be no more than acquaintances, but these people - not friends but not strangers - enrich our lives.

During COVID, people in friendship circles because of a shared experience - parents of kids in the same school, actors in a play, retirement home residents - created pods. That is, groups of people they could depend on to maintain safe practices to avoid the virus. Others formed groups online, or increased outreach in existing groups, to fight the fear and loneliness so prevalent in those early days.

But not since the early days of AIDS did we see such dramatic examples of how little power people had to support, contact or mourn their friends. The first fifteen years of AIDS – 1981-1996 – were pre-social media. We were limited in how we kept in touch with our friends, especially if they did not live nearby.

For many of us working in that community, a pattern emerged.

You'd wake up one day and realize you hadn't seen or heard from one of your friends for a while. You'd ask around and find out that no one else had, either. Not long after, you'd see their face again: on the obituary page of the local LGBT newspaper. People got sick and died alone, a forced isolation fueled by fear and ignorance and stigma. If they lingered for weeks or months, you might have an opportunity to visit them, help out in some way, or say your final goodbyes.

Experiencing those sudden disappearances during COVID, mysteries until you learned your friends had died, was all too familiar to those affected by HIV/AIDS, especially long-term survivors. It was understandable that they'd be triggered by a frightening, unstoppable virus once again raging in their communities. In a later chapter, I'll discuss how they faced it.

When COVID hit, hospitals and nursing homes quickly limited patient access to designated family members, and then only by phone and video. Funeral homes set limits of as few as 10 people for viewings and burials. That meant that even immediate family members might not be able to attend, because the designated ten included funeral workers. Friends were almost always shut out.

"In my faith of Judaism, everything is mandated to occur in a specific way," says [Dr. Joy] Miller. "At a specific time, with a specific prayer. I always knew what to do. Right now, I would normally be at the visitation, making food for the family, standing at the graveside and helping put dirt on the grave until each particle covered my friend completely. I would say Kaddish, and I would mourn, and in eleven months we would return to once again celebrate his life, and place the stone on his grave. But now I can do none of that."[5]

We live in an era where we have online friends around the world, people we've never met in person. But we stay connected with them on Facebook and other platforms because we share something: philosophy, affiliations, passions, interests. Even before the pandemic, it was common to learn of a friend's death in a Facebook post by a family member. It's shocking and painful, but it's helpful to remember one thing: very few people are aware of all the friends their loved one has in their lives, much less online. How could they possibly know who to reach out to? And when the person who died has hundreds, even thousands of social media connections, it's impossible to contact them all individually.

Sharing the news of someone who died became harder during COVID's early days, if they were not on social media. It was almost three weeks after the fact when I received a card alerting me of the death of my late father's best friend; neither he nor his partner were active on any social media platform. And while it was less jarring than seeing the news pop up in my Facebook feed, it was still painful.

There are those who believe that family members are all that matters, that friends are way down the ladder in importance. Sometimes those friends are deliberately denied updates and access, something that was all too common in the early days of AIDS. I was lucky that my friend Christy and her sister kept me informed. I was blindsided enough by other friends' deaths.

If anything defines the frustration of the early days of COVID, it was the desire to do something that could make a difference - maybe even save someone's life, without risking your own. But confusion, the lack of accurate information, and a steep learning curve, all added to that inaction and frustration.

That week of March 10, 2020, I was in New York. I saw only a few friends. We were all trying to figure out what was going on medically and what contact was safe. In those very early COVID days, when masks were not available or even encouraged, we struggled to figure out how to behave. "Do you think it's okay to hug?" one friend asked me. Another simply refused to hug. Yet another wasn't worried about the risk. The city shut down around us - Broadway, museums, sporting events - in a matter of days. Hotels and restaurants emptied out. Panic buying began in the grocery stores.

New York City subway station, undated.

As we became cut off physically, people had to find other ways to support their friends, especially the ones most isolated or under stress.

The pandemic slowed us down and found us returning to old-school methods of keeping in touch. We again used our phones to talk instead of typically texting. When physically isolated, the sound of a friend's voice had the power to conquer loneliness, if only for a few minutes. We relied on FaceTime to assure us of a friend's health. The greeting card industry, which saw 2019 sales register about 50% of that in 2009, now saw a dramatic increase. Despite the closing of greeting card stores deemed non-essential, 76% of adults in the US bought greeting cards in 2020. Sales were up, fueled by millennials suddenly sending cards. Why?

First, not everyone has access to a computer, dependable internet, or a smartphone. That includes not only the elderly or rural residents, but those who are disabled or poor. The good news was that all of them could receive snail mail. Retailers ensured that cards could be purchased online and sent to the customer to personalize and mail; even stamps could be purchased online and delivered to your home. It quickly became a way for friends to keep in touch, bypassing the impersonal, often challenging.

Many card makers began producing pandemic-themed cards in March, and have seen sales creep up as the virus — and its attending isolation — dragged on. At Paper Source, bulk orders are on the rise. "It's a shift in behavior," Ms. Park said. "More people are taking the time to send cards and tell people, 'I care about you.'...It shows we value connection, and we won't take it for granted," she said. "If that's a silver lining coming out of this pandemic, then that's a good one."[6]

2020 Christmas card, PaperSource.com

Friendships are built on both circumstance and luck. All friendships are not equal, or we would honor them all with the title of 'best friend.' We may depend on people for different things, and we continued to depend on them during COVID.

> "We don't always appreciate the symbolic position we occupy in each other's lives until the moment all of that shared history and intimacy comes knocking on our doors. This is why we look up old childhood friends to see where the arc of the plot has led. This is why we often experience a close friend's losses almost as if they were our own: When we bear witness to another life to a degree that they come to feel like an alternate self, a moral responsibility comes attached."[7]

I know I did my part to keep card companies and the post office in business. I made those calls, too. Like many of my friends, the risk of losing touch during a pandemic triggered haunting memories of the early days of HIV/AIDS.

A similar thing happened with COVID. For most people, it was a new and unsettling experience. How do you measure the potential danger of seeing your friends face to face, sharing a meal, or sitting on the same park bench? Do these people mean enough to make that a risk worth taking?

A group of us, all neighbors on one block on the east side of our Chicago street, began to gather for cocktails in the summer of 2020. That sounds a lot more fancy than the reality: four or five couples hanging out on the sidewalk with their own drinks, often entertained by the two young sons of one couple as they raced their mini-ATVs from the alley to the opposite corner. Most of us wore masks. But over time, it was just some of us, then only my husband and I who wore masks. Once or twice a police squad car drove by while we gathered. We knew they were looking for groups to break up if they were violating these new, often confusing restrictions on outdoor gatherings. We were not hassled; I guess we were not the demographic they were looking for. These gatherings - along with a few backyard parties - were free of any complications. In January of 2022, our next-door neighbor died from cancer. My husband took some food over to their house, as family members were arriving from out of town. But he and I did not attend the funeral, unsure if the church would be strict about masking.

It was hard to keep track of some people in those early days of COVID, especially if they left town. It was a phenomenon first reported in New York City, as families retreated from their high-rise apartments to the homes they owned in Bucks County or the Hudson Valley. That, of course, was when we thought the COVID emergency would never last past the summer. They were working from home, and their kids were attending school remotely, so nothing was keeping them in the city. They rented and bought homes in smaller communities they deemed safer than the densely packed city they left behind. But they were oblivious to the strain caused by a dramatic influx of new residents. Housing prices soared. Wealthy new residents demanded products and services they were accustomed to in the city, but not easily available in these new locales, owing to supply chain issues. Most people, of course, did not have the means to relocate. And many friends felt abandoned, left to the risks of remaining behind in a hot zone, perhaps left to die.

People whose jobs were classified as essential were least likely to be able to work from home. That group included those on the front lines in medical facilities, but also people who fought fires, drove buses, stocked groceries, and delivered anything and everything to people who had the luxury of working from home. You may have felt virtuous for quarantining, but your delivery driver assumed your risk.

We became friends with those essential workers, the ones delivering your Amazon Prime orders, in part because they were often the only people we saw on a regular basis.

Maybe not friends like your BFF, but someone we got to know a little better; someone we wanted to show appreciation to for doing a job few sought. And like those early days of AIDS, if they disappeared even for a few days, we became unsettled.

I'm a creature of habit, so I eat at the same two or three diners on any trip to New York City. When I returned there in May 2021, for the first time in fourteen months, I wondered if two of my favorite servers would still be there. When I walked into their respective diners and didn't see them, I told myself they were working a different shift. That was true for one of them, who I finally saw on my second trip at her diner, a working mom working on Mother's Day. That day, I tipped her 50%. Though it had been over a year, she remembered me and seemed genuinely happy that I was back. That was a real hallmark of these reunions with all kinds of friends: a palpable relief sometimes intense enough to bring on tears. I never saw the other server, even after a few return visits to his diner. He was older, around my age, and a huge flirt. I was afraid to ask about him, so I prefer to believe he retired.

The hugs, when we did finally gather with friends again, became longer and tighter than before COVID. The hugs were not just for the relief and joy of being together again, but to make up for what we had experienced: "I'm sorry for what you've gone through. I wish I could have helped you more." And always, it was to acknowledge that we were still standing, even if other friends were no longer with us.

I have more of my friends' phone numbers in my phone than I did before COVID. That's because, early on, a few friends insisted on exchanging numbers. We'd always communicated via Facebook or Twitter or email; phone calls and even texting seemed unnecessary. But there was an urgency that you might describe as panic, a need to make sure we would not lose touch.

In 2023, I conducted a very unscientific survey on Facebook; I asked people how they kept in touch with friends during COVID. The same way they always had? Same frequency of contact? What did they do more of? Or did they now connect in a different way? The results were very telling:

"For about 18 months, my only in-person contact with others was grocery shopping."

> "...had a list of specific friends who were in the 'newish' levels of friendship development and made calendar reminders to check in and set dates to meet outdoors and do garden walks, etc., to keep

building relationships and not have them fall by the wayside."

"Lots of Zooming and other videoconferencing. The most regular one, and which has continued, is a weekly Facebook Messenger video call with a group of college friends. Seven of us, spread over Illinois, Tennessee, Florida, Israel and (for me) California and then Oregon. Used to do it every Saturday, recently moved it to Sunday. Since the pandemic abated, not all of us make it every week, but most of us do."

"Zoom zoom zoom. It's much easier for us on the autism spectrum to endure isolation. We reach out in a DM or Zoom when we feel we have something pertinent to share so for us, it's mostly the same old same old routine."[8]

Facebook, and in different ways, Twitter, became a kind of town square where people gathered and checked in: "Have you heard from Sharon? Does anyone know if Peter is still in town?" Sometimes alarms were sounded, when normally extroverted friends fell silent, or when messages went unreturned. That's probably why, especially during COVID, we've been shocked time and again by announcements on Facebook about someone who died. It will never not be jarring to see the news of a friend's death pop up in your newsfeed.

Because we were friends and not family, we were not privy to personal medical information that wasn't pro-actively shared. Hospitals would not give us information on our friends, and we certainly could not visit them during COVID.

"Does anyone know anyone at Memorial Sloan Kettering? At St. John's? At Northwestern?" We worked our contacts as furiously as if we were job-hunting. But this time we were friend-hunting.

Why was all that necessary? Why not just reach out to their families?

There's a reason why not. I can guarantee that you've never met the families of many of your friends, and that your family doesn't know more than a small fraction of your friends. They don't know about your friend from grad school who moved to Portland, or your former work buddy who retired to Tennessee. They don't know you have friendships that exist only on social media, be-cause you've never actually met those people in person. It's a strange phenomenon. Social media instantly brings people together from all over the world, but in a crisis, they can be hard to reach. And again, without knowing every one of the deceased, families must resort to these public announcements.

Keeping in touch with friends, whether those you see in person on a regular basis, or others who are far-flung, is hard. Keeping in touch during a pandemic, then, became a challenge. You may have even felt at times that it was too much work. One thing that made it a little easier, for better or worse, was politics.

The first ten months of COVID would've been traumatic enough if that had been the only challenge we faced. But think of what else was going on between March 2020 and January 2021:

- Presidential primaries
- George Floyd was murdered
- General election
- January 6 insurrection
- Inauguration Day

Some of our friendships had been fraying for years already when COVID shut down our world. Some of them had already been abandoned. But toxic politics hastened the demise of other friendships during the period when COVID hit.

No friendship exists without disagreements, especially those that have lasted for decades. We never agree on everything, whether it's music or food or fashion. But now, those years-long decisions to 'agree to disagree' about politics no longer made sense, when the people we disagreed with had already decided publicly online that whole groups of people deserved to die. For those of us with history in the HIV/AIDS community, this was all too familiar.

As I talked to friends throughout the COVID pandemic, this was often the thing that broke them: not nonsensical pronouncements from the White House, or loss of income or even racial violence. It was the idea that people they knew, people they long considered friends, were willing to write off the lives of others to offset their own inconveniences.

Maybe we would've tired of agreeing to disagree without COVID. Maybe we would have continued to convince ourselves that these friends were good people at heart, who were just temporarily misguided.

Or maybe we would have still been changed forever:

When it was over, they no longer greeted each other by shaking hands, though their hands were cleaner than ever. They hugged fewer people now, but most could not resist hugging the ones they loved; they wept to feel the pulse and warmth of the bodies they had missed so deeply. Others continued to keep their distance, and simply placed their hands over their hearts and bowed.

Some gathered for overdue mourning in honor of those who had died. So many had died. When it was over, the living understood more about death.

...Yes, the people were sad, but in some ways happier, or at least wiser, than before.

Why had it taken so much pain for them to clearly see what and who they loved? To appreciate a slower life? To reconnect with old friends?

...'We'll never take so much for granted again,' they said. A few of them kept the promise.[9]

On Sundays, a Clergy Collar and a Hazmat Suit

The ability to be and to have friends
is all a part of that to which Loretto calls us.
It requires of us an open spirit and a sensitive,
loving attention to one another. It requires a heart.[1]

For thousands of years, people have turned to their faith traditions for comfort and support. They realized that familiar rituals they grew up with reassure them in a world filled with fear and uncertainty.

Daoud Nassimi is a volunteer imam in a northern Virginia suburb. He witnessed first-hand the pain of those unable during COVID to conduct normal funeral rituals: ritual washing of the body, wrapping the deceased in a kaffan (shroud), then burial within 24 hours, usually without a casket. While acknowledging the distress caused by the interruption of religious practices, he assured his community that changes could be made. The tenets of Islam can accommodate extraordinary circumstances like pandemics, assuaging the guilt of being unable to follow tradition.

Leaders of faith communities follow what they believe to be a deep, spiritual calling. Part of that mission is creating connections with their congregants, many of whom become friends. When COVID struck, people looked to their religious leaders for guidance and hope. But those leaders were also living through the same frightening time, one that not only affected how they conducted their ministries, but how they navigated their personal lives.

Rev. Neil Pfeifer is the pastor of St. Philip Neri parish in Napoleon, N.D. The COVID crisis forced him to cancel in-person Easter services in 2020. That loss of shared experience inspired the pastor to focus on online masses, eventually drawing 1,500 viewers a week. In October of that year, a teenage parishioner died from suicide, a death that weighed on him because of his inability at the time to counsel people in person. A week later, one of his close friends, Msgr. Jeffrey Wald, died from COVID. Pfeifer was notified of the death on the same day he personally tested positive for the virus.

"For me to be home during his funeral and planning, it was a really difficult time," Pfeifer says, adding that prayer and spiritual direction provided solace. "We need others," he adds, noting that even pastors need to be pastored at times.[2]

The lead pastor at Plymouth Church in downtown Seattle, Dr. Rev. Kelle Brown ministers to an older congregation that was uniquely vulnerable to COVID. Like her parishioners, she, too, often found herself in tears because she had no idea if she was doing things the right way.

"I've felt handicapped and as if someone had cut off bits of me because I didn't feel like I could do what I normally do. I wasn't able to pastor and minister; I wasn't able to be a friend...I wasn't able to extend compassion in the normal ways...And it's so crushing to walk with people, to companion people through illness, virtually."[3]

Rev. Brown realized she needed to pay attention to her own sorrow, so that she could be of use to others. She created a simple, daily ritual: lighting a candle. To her it represented an abundance of love for every person, with the dripping wax signifying the tears "that are so necessary to get us through this time."

"Every day that I light the candle I feel its heat. I am reminded that that's how it will feel when I'm able to hug friends and family again that I'm missing. And together, all of us are feeling the heat of our flames. We know that we will be different on the other side of it, but we will be. And that's going to be enough."[4]

Members of religious congregations, be they priests, ministers, imams, nuns, or rabbis, not only live with their own pain, but their community's pain. Yet COVID amplified divisions that already existed. Still these people were expected to love and minister even to those who disagree with them. They were already struggling to minister when George Floyd was murdered, and as pre-election rhetoric stoked simmering tensions. Relationships in many congregations were already strained by race and politics. For many, COVID was their breaking point.

Tish Harrison Warren, an Anglican priest, reflected on this in the *New York Times* in August of 2022:

"Shawn [McCain Tirres, her friend and rector of her church] is one of the most lighthearted people I know, constantly laughing and joking. But, over the past year, he realized that he had grown deeply angry, as he put it, 'not only with people and issues and society but with God.' When I asked him what he was angry about, his voice broke. He was quiet for a long time and then said through tears, 'Losing Bill the way we did. That's a big one.' Bill was a member of our church who died of COVID after contracting it in his nursing home. Unable to visit Bill because of hospital protocols, Shawn couldn't be by his side. He gave his friend last rites over FaceTime."[5]

Rector of the Cathedral of the Sacred Heart livestreams the Stations of the Cross on Good Friday, Catholic Diocese of Richmond, VA, April 10, 2020.

The technological learning curve was steep for religious leaders. Regardless of their age, the same issues had to be considered: did everyone in the congregation have computers or smartphones and access to reliable internet service? Did they have the capability to offer closed-captioning for the hearing-impaired? What parts of their services had to be adapted or eliminated to virtual worship? Was recording the worship an option? The forced isolation deeply frustrated their ability to minister to their congregations. The concerns of an Indiana pastor echoed those felt by teachers and doctors:

> "I never got tired of pastoring or thinking about Scripture and preaching," she said. "I just started associating ministry with having to learn new computer programs and having embarrassing, anxious moments around technology." She continued, "Over time, pastoral ministry started to seem like a total absurdity. The world around me was on fire and I was stuck in an empty church building figuring out Zoom."[6]

COVID restrictions meant that most regular religious practices had to be canceled or modified: no giving out of communion, no sharing the 'kiss of peace,' no sitting shiva. The sense of community embodied by a congregation of unrelated people was put on hold. The experience of worshiping together did not have the same power when transmitted over the internet. And while those gathered to worship typically look to their congregants for leadership, those leaders were also suffering a profound sense of loss and frustration. They had few answers. Those losses were not only between religious and lay people; they were also felt within religious communities.

The average age of a Catholic nun in the US is almost 80. And the number of nuns overall has dropped from almost 200,000 in 1965 to about 40,000 in 2020. Given those demographics, the leadership of their congregations knew that COVID was likely to have a devastating effect, further diminishing the dwindling number of nuns.

The Leadership Conference of Women Religious agreed to hold their August 2020 assembly on Zoom. LCWR members are leaders of religious orders representing 80% of Catholic nuns in the US. Holding an online meeting for a few dozen people was already a challenge. Their first assembly during COVID welcomed 1,000 participants. They confronted the same challenge as funeral directors and pastors: how to bring people together virtually while still allowing for privacy and spiritual communion. That first virtual assembly, significantly, allowed these women leaders to grieve.

One panel discussion, "Grief as a Catalyst for Transformation and Hope," was followed by small breakout groups to discuss the "transformational potential of their individual and mutual grief." Sr. Maureen Geary, a Dominican sister from Grand Rapids, Michigan, opened the panel with a focus on the importance of being present in the 'permanent now' that they were all forced into.

> Geary recalled the image of the women sitting faithfully next to Jesus' tomb, the stone still in place before the eventual miracle. In their waiting, they were 'present to their now,' said Geary.

> 'The space that grief creates is where God works transformation. For me this seems a slow transformation, and very incomplete. But I am being transformed, a little more each day in another permanent now,' sitting by the 'tombs of our day,' looking for the light that seeps through the cracks between the stones.[7]

For another panelist, Maryknoll Sr. Antoinette Gutzler from Queens, New York, the inability to hold a funeral or wake was especially devastating, since fourteen sisters in her community died in the first five months of COVID.

'A grief began to settle over me, a wrenching experience of learning to live and to let go in this unprecedented time,' she said. 'My tears are still close to the surface, but never shed for fear they may not stop.'[8]

Not all of those deaths were the result of COVID, but the restrictions were the same.

'[Some sisters feel] re-traumatized every time you experience another death, because the first one has not yet been put to rest,' said Sr. Sean Peters, a Sister of St. Joseph of Carondelet.[9]

Like the ministers whose stories were shared earlier, the nuns like Sr. Kathy Stein looked for ways to channel their grief for members, as well as for the world at large.

Through the pain of not being able to pray together, 'we've realized how important that relationship is, and new ways that that can happen.' In letting go of ministries, she said, they can now focus on mission, and how 'no matter where we are or what we're doing, as we move into the future, our mission is alive and well.'[10].

A year later, LCWR held their second virtual assembly. But this time, rather than just a series of standard Zoom plenaries and breakout sessions, it was structured as a religious retreat for 1,300 women, run by over 100 volunteers. Deborah Asberry of Community Works, who served as the assembly's facilitator, said that format was a deliberate "response to the stress and trauma that leaders of congregations have experienced in the last 18 months." And while none of the attendees compared their own trauma to that experienced by those to whom they minister, there were unique challenges.

Where the norm had been for all nuns to live in a convent, most now live in different group settings. Sr. Helen Santamaria is a Sister of Loretto, an order founded in Kentucky in 1812. A nun for 60 years, she is as joyful and focused as she was when I first met her my freshman year of high school in 1966. Her vitality was still in evidence when we spoke in December of 2022 about her needs during COVID while living in a less-traditional setting.

*Sr. Helen Santamaria, undated photo,
permission of Loretto Community*

Sr. Helen lives in one of three apartments in a bungalow on the grounds of the former Loretto Academy in El Paso, which formerly housed the home economics department. Only one of the four people in the house was affected by COVID. They were all very serious about quarantine. Someone else went to the grocery store for Sr. Helen. Her only visitor was the executive director of the opportunity center for the homeless.

The sacrament of holy communion is part of Catholic tradition. A sacred part of every mass, it is not a requirement, though the Church expects Catholics to receive communion at least once a year. Less than half of American Catholics report always taking communion at mass. But for some, daily communion, whether or not a part of mass, is an important element of their faith. Sr. Helen's visitor was one of those people. He was a daily communicant, and with the cathedral closed to visitors, was unable to continue this practice. So, she offered to step in until he was able to resume his normal practice.

Sr. Helen lost many friends to COVID. The Loretto motherhouse in Kentucky is located just down a winding road from Thomas Merton's Gethsemane. The motherhouse is one of the largest employers in the area. Despite their efforts at isolating and canceling communal meals and prayers, COVID broke through; between March 2020 and August 2022, 29 nuns died. By The end of the year, eighty were left.

Like Sr. Helen, Jan Hayes, a Sister of Mercy of the Americas, also lives less traditionally.

Sister Jan lives in an apartment building in south St. Louis, rooming with two other Sisters of Mercy, one Adrian Dominican nun and two lay people. Each has her own apartment but they eat and pray together. They have neighbors in the building, both married and single.

COVID upended their worship routine, forcing them to Zoom prayer meetings, even though they lived in the same building. That, to Sr. Jan, was the hardest adjustment. She and another nun worked outside the home and worried about spreading COVID to fellow residents. Those precautions lasted until April 2021, when all were vaccinated.

Sr. Jan teaches undergraduate courses in Media Ethics and Media & Social Justice at Webster University, whose classes and administration went fully remote following the outbreak of COVID in March 2020. "The teacher became the student," she laughed, citing how she was forced to adapt her teaching for live-streaming. That fall, they were back in the classroom with strict guidelines - wearing masks, sanitizing desks, etc. Despite grumbling when vaccines were later mandated, her students complied, so she avoided contracting COVID.

She admits that traditional religious retirement settings had it worse. They went through a cycle of shutting down and opening up, only to shut down again. They tended to err on the side of caution, given the ages of the nuns.

Sr. Carol Zinn, of the Leadership of Women Religious, noted what Sr. Jan experienced: "There was the absence of common meals, common prayer, common liturgy, all the celebrations of life, of jubilees and funerals."[11]

Though no one in her apartment building died, other nuns in their congregation did, from COVID and other causes. No one could visit them when they were dying, nor attend their funerals. It took up to eight months for ceremonies to go digital, which was an improvement but a poor substitute for gathering in person to honor the women they served with for decades. Some communities delayed in-person funerals altogether until there was enough of a downturn in COVID to safely gather.

But no matter the constraints, Sister Jan felt that all nuns gained a realization of how much they cared about each other, a willingness to adapt so that their bonds would not be broken. She senses a new resilience in herself, as well as a change in her personal faith.

"My faith has been hardened, tested, maybe more realistic now." [12]

The day after we spoke, Sr. Jan emailed me. She'd just returned from the funeral of Sr. Michaelanne, who'd died a month earlier. Her funeral had been delayed because of a COVID spike, and being together to "laugh, cry, share memories...was a relief."

Adapting to the pandemic meant more than just learning how to conduct services online. When I started this book, I assumed the people in this chapter would describe experiencing a crisis of faith: a questioning of their belief in God or their faith traditions. Perhaps they felt God was absent from the horrors of the pandemic. Those I interviewed freely admitted to feeling frustrated, depressed, frightened and angry, helpless in the face of so much loss. But none admitted totally losing their faith. I did not expect all of them to affirm that their faith had been strengthened by COVID.

> "Do I understand why this happened? No. But it didn't diminish my faith. It was a joy to communicate that. I see 26 people once a month. It was a privilege to say that. We have to trust. God brought me to be a spiritual director at this time." - [13]

Charles King holds both law and divinity degrees from Yale. He is also CEO and co-founder of Housing Works in New York City. An offshoot of the housing committee of ACT UP/NY (AIDS Coalition to Unleash Power), the organization has been helping homeless people living with HIV/AIDS since 1990. They provide a full range of services including housing, health care, mental health, and chemical dependency services for homeless men, women, and children living with HIV/AIDS and other chronic conditions.

Those dark, early days of HIV/AIDS echoed in the beginning of COVID, which will be explained in more depth in a later chapter. This new, frightening virus that killed otherwise healthy individuals in horrific ways led to rampant discrimination.

Charles King is also a Baptist minister, in addition to his bureaucratic and advocacy duties. King "puts on his collar," as he describes it, and leads funeral services.

Charles King, undated photo,
permission of Housing Works

New York was hit early and hard by COVID, which was devastating to a minority urban population already suffering from medical and systemic neglect. Homeless shelter providers were instructed to screen residents for COVID if they had symptoms. Because test results took three days, they were not allowed to return to the shelters until they had a negative result test. Homeless people who had been treated in the hospital were released to the streets because there was no place to quarantine.

Tourists fled the city, leaving hotels empty. Some buildings were converted temporarily to house the homeless, a safer option than crowded shelters ill-equipped to protect them from COVID. City services needed by people without housing, however, were suspended or lacking.

The challenges faced by Housing Works were the most serious in decades, on a par with the early 1990s, before the antiretroviral cocktail gave hope to people with HIV/AIDS. King's energy was focused on the immediate crisis: scrambling to acquire PPE for his staff and clients, finding safe alternatives to city shelters and continuing the care the clients depended on. But he also had to provide spiritual support to clients.

By April 2020, King was presiding over at least one or two memorials a week, making him recall the worst days of the HIV/AIDS epidemic. It wasn't just COVID deaths. Housing Works was already seeing a higher rate of overdose deaths during COVID, as well as suicides and illnesses in clients suffering from addiction and multiple health complications. The inability to access medical care during COVID, along with isolation and depression, were surely contributing factors, King said.

In the first eighteen months of the pandemic, between March 2020 and October 2021, King conducted 67 memorial services for clients and colleagues. King only felt a couple of instances of personal COVID panic during that time.

One occurred in June 2021, when King gave the eulogy for an older man with HIV and other conditions, who died from COVID. He had never given such an angry eulogy. He kept asking himself, "Why didn't we vaccinate him in January? I don't know if he chose not to be vaccinated. "

He felt profoundly depressed after that service.

> The realization that I was going to see people I cared about die, even after the vaccine, was depressing. Others hurt more because they were closer.
>
> I find it very healing to go through the process of constructing eulogies. I feel more thoughtful doing them. I used to just walk in with a scripture chosen, nothing else. But I didn't want them to sound the same. Now, I'm actually writing out a eulogy, adding a reading or poem that matches who that person is.[14]

Did any of the people of faith in this chapter have pat answers stemming from their religious dogma? No. Did that surprise you? Their faith did not immunize them against doubt or anger or despair in the age of COVID. They struggled to find meaning in a worldwide pandemic, just as we all did. Their friends, as well as their congregations, sought answers they found they could not easily provide. They struggled and grieved alongside the people they led but kept going.

"This is what it must be like in a warzone."

Colleagues don't die like this.[1]

"First, do no harm" is recognized by many people as being part of the Hippocratic oath. It's a promise made by doctors to act only in the interest of their patients, to seek healthy outcomes and not prolong suffering. But in those early months of COVID, routine treatment plans had to be abandoned for a simple reason: the virus was stronger than the conventional tools they had to work with. The medical challenges COVID posed were unprecedented, complicated by politics, race and indifference. The toll that it took on the medical world will be discussed later.

But I want to first address the logistics the medical world faced in providing care during COVID.

It seemed as if recommended treatments and precautions changed from day to day. America's information primarily came from the National Institutes of Health, with Dr. Anthony Fauci briefing the public, and from Trump's White House, desperate to downplay the severity of the pandemic by alternately dismissing the advice of experts and promoting wild, unproven treatments. Those two sources regularly contradicted each other. One well-known example of that confusion was the recommendation of hydroxychloroquine sulfate.

When COVID first hit in March 2020, researchers hoped that existing antiretroviral treatments would be effective against this new virus. Hydroxychloroquine was one of them, based on a very small study. But by June, the FDA had reversed its position on the drug, based on new evidence citing ineffectiveness and a danger of heart complications that could be potentially fatal.

But because the drug had once offered hope, however small, media celebrities like Fox News' Laura Ingraham and talk show host Dr. Mehmet Oz, continued to promote it to their followers. Peter Navarro, aide to President Trump, pressured the FDA to reauthorize it. There is no evidence that the FDA caved to pressure, but the damage had already been done.

COVID patients were now demanding hydroxychloroquine in hospitals. They were willing to sue for access, and some did.

That was not the only unproven drug that patients demanded.

Another was ivermectin, normally prescribed by veterinarians to treat parasitic infections in animals. In very limited situations - such as head lice or river blindness - it is effective in humans. It was never approved by the FDA for treating or preventing COVID, but that did not stop politicians and celebrities from promoting it to a population desperate for solutions. Veterinarians and farmers were suddenly unable to find the drug since people were taking it on their own without medical supervision. Poison control centers reported a three-fold increase in distress calls related to Ivermectin in the first year of the pandemic.

The FDA, NIH, infectious disease specialists and epidemiologists did not have the answers, nor answers that remained effective. It often seemed like they were guessing. Their guessing, though, was based on decades of experience and research being conducted at lightning speed, not quackery or get-rich-quick schemes. But for people whose loved ones were in pain or dying alone, any glimmer of hope was something to grab. For front-line medical workers, the frequent policy changes in treatment advice were hard enough to manage. The rampant medical disinformation made it even harder.

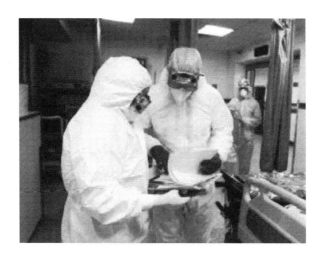

Unidentified hospital workers, March, 2020,
blog post on victorianoe.com

At the same time, critically important medical equipment, like ventilators, were in limited supply. The public was desperate to find masks and gaiters, though we were initially ordered to not purchase masks because they were needed in hospitals and nursing homes. Meanwhile, in those hospitals, personal protective equipment was rationed. Disposable surgical masks, not meant to be reused, were being worn for days at a time. Plastic garbage bags were used when hospital gowns ran out. The shortages meant that unprepared hospital administrators - and often the desperate frontline staff themselves - were begging the public for help. They bid against each other online for supplies because the White House told each state they should not expect a federalized response to purchasing. That resulted in state governments and individual facilities paying exorbitant prices to greedy companies, and falling victim to scam artists. Millions of dollars were wasted on PPE that was never delivered, because the federal government hijacked orders placed by state governments – orders that were redirected or simply disappeared. That left administrators frustrated and frontline workers even more at risk.

In April 2020, Rhonda Roland Shearer helped create Cut Red Tape 4 Heroes, a partnership with the New York City-based Housing Works, on whose board she serves. She had first begun providing gloves and face masks to people working on 'the pile' after 9/11. This time, she tried first to work deals she could pass on to city agencies. But frustrated by slow-moving and inefficient bureaucracies, she decided to distribute supplies directly. She took out a $600,000 home equity loan to buy and disseminate PPE to desperate hospital workers and the homeless.

Some hospitals, determined to prove that they could provide needed equipment to their employees, refused donations of PPE. They even prohibited her from setting up her distribution stations on hospital property. Instead Shearer moved across the street, displaying signage for frontline workers to take her free supplies.

In the absence of available medical-grade masks, the public turned to cloth masks. Companies and individuals were soon making their own, often giving them away for free. Were they as effective? In the short term, they opened up the flow of disposable masks for front-line workers. Cloth masks were reusable and certainly better than nothing, though subsequent variants of the virus rendered them less effective than compared to N95 masks. Nonprofits sold masks as a way of generating income. Everything from works of art to political statements appeared on masks. Cloth masks became a fashion trend as well. House Speaker Nancy Pelosi coordinated her masks to her outfits. With people focused on building a wardrobe of masks, the shortage on the front lines eased.

Due to unprecedented numbers of critically ill patients, hospitals found themselves faced with a shortage of staff. Doctors, nurses and technicians. normally assigned to departments that are not crisis-oriented, were moved to the internal medicine and emergency departments to supplement exhausted front-line workers. Because of their experience, they did not require supervision, but it was quickly evident that they were a short-term fix.

Fortunately, the pandemic occurred at a time when medical students were close to spring graduation. Dr. Steven Abramson, vice dean for academic affairs at New York University medical school, began receiving emails in March 2020, from fourth-year students who wanted to help the medical workers who had trained them at Bellevue and Tisch. After all, they'd completed all their class requirements and were just waiting for graduation. Abramson sent out a survey asking if students would be willing to begin their residencies early. They would not be matched to their specialties; all would be assigned to the overworked internal medicine units for the short term. Within twelve hours, more than half agreed. So NYU applied for state approval for early graduation, followed soon after by Mount Sinai, Columbia, and Albert Einstein School of Medicine.

Fourth-year medical students weren't walking into a hospital for the first time but are typically supervised. It was not an ideal situation, but it was a crucial tactic to meet the patient load. The first advisory from the Association of American Medical Colleges (AAMC) came on March 17: pull all students out of the classroom and put them on the floors. There was no precedent for this in our lifetimes. The last time medical students were graduated early was in response to the 1918 Spanish Flu epidemic.

It was a sign of an inherent weakness in our public health system. Hospitals are set up to respond to time-limited disasters: hurricanes, mass shootings, building collapses. Not a pandemic with no end in sight.

In the 2021 book *Life on the Line: Young Doctors Come of Age in a Pandemic,* author Emma Goldberg follows six of these fourth-year medical students in New York City during the first months of COVID. The new doctors quickly come face to face with the challenges of taking care of their patients and processing the grief that hung over everything.

> Iris arrived at 7:00 on Friday morning, anxious to check in with the night team about how Mr. Lopez had fared overnight. As they gathered, the night nurse gave Iris a look she recognized...
>
> 'We have some unfortunate news', the nurse said. She turned to Iris. 'Mr. Lopez passed away last night.'
>
> 'Let's take thirty seconds of silence,' the attending physician said.

Standing at the nurses' station, Iris suddenly wondered whether she had made a mistake coming here... She felt overpowered by a blistering sense of loss - but shouldn't she have been more emotionally prepared?

...This was Iris's first time losing her own patient. She bit her lip, steadied her breath. Then the moment of silence broke. The night team continued with their handover notes.[2]

Remember that not all patients were there because of COVID. Ben, another four-year student followed by Goldberg, was assigned several newly-admitted patients his first week. One of them, Mr. Moore, had suffered a heart attack the night before, but was alert and stable. Before Ben went to dinner, he put Mr. Moore on the phone with his daughter. While eating the pizza sent by a local parlor, Ben heard a rapid response alert for his floor over the PA system. A resident offered to check on it. When the resident didn't return, Ben raced up to Mr. Moore's room but the patient was already dead.

On top of the shock, Ben realized that the next steps were his responsibility: contacting the family, and advising on what funeral parlors might handle the burial. And though Ben and his team had done everything they could for the patient, he realized that would be of little consolation to his survivors.

Just a few months after COVID hit the US, in May of 2020, racial issues came to the forefront with the murder of George Floyd. Our society was forced again to confront decades of police brutality and racial injustice, now on full, horrifying display in the video of Floyd's murder in police custody. Marches and demonstrations around the country resulted, some planned, many spontaneous. The Republican administration described the marchers as violent thugs, though violence was rare - and some of it was prompted by rogue cops or right-wing agitators. Not everyone who wanted to march did, because that summer America still struggled to determine if outdoor gatherings of thousands of people in close proximity could create what became known as super-spreader events. The outrage in the streets was deeply felt by the medical staff.

Filmmaker Matthew Heineman's 2021 Emmy-nominated documentary *The First Wave* is a fascinating and horrifying record of the early days of the pandemic. It was filmed during the first months of COVID at Long Island Jewish Medical Center, one of the hardest-hit hospitals at the epicenter of the outbreak. There are no talking heads, no outside experts interpreting what you're watching. Viewers find themselves following two patients and several front-line workers as they bear witness to challenges every day for months. In the film, Dr. Nathalie Dougé, a first-generation Haitian-American internal medicine specialist, is the moral center of a harrowing journey. It begins with a patient dying - a patient who, just minutes earlier, had been chatting with their family on an iPad. That opening sequence is indicative of what millions of medical professionals faced during COVID.

The film explores the mechanics of keeping patients breathing and alive, as well as the personalities and passion of the frontline workers. We learn about Dr. Dougé's love of singer Lionel Richie, and witness those precious moments when doctors and nurses struggle to understand how their patients – sitting up and talking – suddenly die minutes later. We see the pandemic through the eyes of people of color – both patients and medical staff – a more accurate representation that was missing from the nightly news reports.

After the murder of George Floyd, Dr. Dougé debated whether to march with other New Yorkers. But the virus still raged, making even outdoor events a vector for transmission. She finally decided to join with thousands of others, masked up in their scrubs, marching and holding a sign that read "Racism is a public health issue." The crowd made its way through New York City streets as they chanted George Floyd's last words: "I can't breathe." As chilling as those words sounded to the public, they resonated much more deeply with Dr. Dougé: those were also the words gasped in terror by her COVID patients, multiple times a day, since the beginning of the pandemic.

In one memorable moment during the march, she witnessed a young Black man confronting a police officer, who was ignoring him. The rage and frustration, not just about Floyd's death, but the pandemic and decades of racism, were boiling over, and she worried that she was about to witness the senseless loss of another Black man. Dr. Dougé stood between him and the officer, to help defuse the situation, telling him, "Your family cares about you." Afterwards, the young man hugged her.

At that moment, the doctor realized it had been months since she'd been hugged. The physical contact she'd experienced from day to day was limited to the life-and-death situations of the workplace. But that incident at the march made Dr. Dougé realize that she had the power to help others beyond her work at the hospital.

*Dr. Thomas Fisher, undated photograph,
Penguin Random House Speakers Bureau*

Meanwhile, in Chicago, Dr. Thomas Fisher worked in the emergency department at the University of Chicago Medical Center, on the city's South Side. In his memoir, *The Emergency: A Year of Healing and Heartbreak in a Chicago ER,* he points out that emergency medicine as we know it only gained importance in the 1970s. It's a very different way of practicing medicine: staff who thrive in a constantly changing environment that some might describe as controlled chaos, people who possess an ability to assess patients quickly and move on to the next case. It's not for everyone. But it's a world he was drawn to.

Like the patients seen in *The First Wave*, Dr. Fisher's patients are overwhelmingly people of color, maybe working class, often poor. COVID, in many ways, was just one more crisis in a long list of challenges his vulnerable patients had to deal with on a daily basis. They were already suffering from chronic illnesses like diabetes, heart disease and COPD; an institutional lack of safe, affordable housing; fewer city services than are easily found in wealthier, white neighborhoods; not to mention the physical and emotional trauma inflicted by the gun violence rampant in their communities. Dr. Fisher reflected on that six months into the pandemic:

> When I finally get back to my home in the West Loop, after I've deposited my scrubs in the laundry and washed off the hospital grime, I walk to the grocery store to replenish my fridge. It's tranquil. Fully stocked, ripe bananas and yogurt on sale. Bearded hipsters in Off-White sneakers buy fresh salmon. Women in $150 yoga pants load up on snacks. If not for masks and a proliferation of plexiglass screens it would seem that everything is normal. But the South Side is not at all normal...Even as I'm

largely protected in my neighborhood, my patients are suffocated by the virus and shot full of holes. Their dead bodies wait to be taken to the morgue while I work, wrapped in plastic and breathing through a filter, to prevent that outcome for others who are febrile and bleeding. Segregation means that on the North Side of town folks can maintain the illusion that things aren't that bad so long as the stock market stays afloat. Straddling these two worlds makes me insane. Is this grocery store real, or is what I've experienced and seen in the hospital real? Because they cannot both be real.

Or can they?[3]

Medical professionals around the country took to the streets, marching to raise visibility about the deadly consequences of racism in the pandemic. They saw the disparities every day, and they were determined that we would, too.

Racial tensions also included a sharp uptick in anti-Asian hate crimes. From the beginning of the pandemic, the president refused to use 'coronavirus' or 'COVID' to describe the virus. He insisted on referring to it as the 'China virus,' accusing a lab in Wuhan of deliberately unleashing the virus on the world. Absorbing Trump's racist dog whistle speeches, people turned their wrath on anyone who looked Asian. It didn't matter if they were of Chinese, Japanese, Korean, Thai, Filipino or Vietnamese descent. They looked Asian, and that was enough to stoke this anger. People even refused to eat at Chinese restaurants.

Nora (not her real name) is a retired hospice medical director and palliative care physician. Nora is Korean-American. She'd been aware of COVID since January of 2020, because of family living in Korea. She was among the tens of thousands who answered Governor Cuomo's call for additional medical personnel to volunteer at New York's overwhelmed hospitals. End-of-life specialists were desperately needed. Death and dying were not new to her. She was used to hard conversations. Normally, decisions were made in a patient's room with their loved ones present; Nora would leave the room so families could make decisions or have final conversations. Being physically present now meant they could see for themselves, not merely the patient, but the tubes and wires and machines. Being in the room made it harder for anyone to be in denial. With COVID eliminating that in-person option, she had to facilitate calls with family members by phone or FaceTime to discuss treatment options, or to resolve a conflict between doctors and patients or their families. The only person in the room with the patient, she was now a witness to these intimate conversations. She held the phone so patients could talk to loved ones, possibly for the last time.

For the first time in her medical career, Nora deliberately wore her scrubs on public transportation to and from work, in defiant response to the rise in anti-Asian sentiment. Maybe people would see that she was part of the solution, not part of the problem. Anti-Asian sentiment did not exist in the workplace; no one refused to work with her. Once at the hospital, suiting up meant not just scrubs and gloves, but visors, surgical masks and layers of coverings. Her face was largely hidden. That advantage allowed her to avoid any bigotry during work with critically ill patients and desperate families.

Her volunteer rotation lasted March and April. She never said no when asked to come in, despite knowing she could refuse. It helped her cope. Hospital staff didn't have that option.

One colleague of Nora, a friend whose wedding she'd attended, died on Easter Sunday at another hospital. Another colleague died later in the spring. Four or five who were in the ICU died while she was on duty. Like soldiers on the battlefield, she had no adequate way to grieve in the moment. All she could do was go into the bathroom and cry.

Kaiser Health News and the *Guardian* reported that in the first year of the pandemic, more than 3,300 nurses, doctors, social workers and physical therapists died from COVID. The Centers for Medicare and Medicaid Services tallied 1,332 fatalities among nursing home workers alone. And though medical professionals make up roughly 4 percent of the general population, according to numerous studies they accounted for 10-20 percent of coronavirus cases in the early months.

It stands to reason that people in such an intimate setting, taking care of people already infected, would be at heightened risk themselves. That is why the stories of inadequate PPE were so horrifying: people who knew the dangers of reusing K95 masks continued to put themselves at risk to take care of people in critical condition. They, like others whose jobs were deemed essential, had no choice but to continue to work. Statistics show that many paid the price for their dedication.

Ben, one of those fourth-year students in New York, heard rumors that a third-year Montefiore emergency medicine resident was in ICU with COVID. Normally possessed of an amount of energy that powered him through many late-night shifts, his colleague was brought down by the virus he was treating in his patients. But he delayed getting treatment because he didn't want to add to the already overwhelming patient load. One of the doctors who admitted him also ran the residency program. Later, he went into his office, put his head down on the desk, and cried.

And then he went back to work.

One of the complications of war is that the people on the battlefield do not have the luxury to grieve in the moment. It's hard enough just to process the bodies of those who have fallen. You can't call a time-out in the midst of a battle to hold a funeral. The same held true for first responders fighting COVID. There was no time to stop what they were doing, not even to mourn those who served alongside them. Pinning cards and photos to a bulletin board behind the front desk was all that was possible to remember colleagues struck down in service.

Much has been made of the people who celebrated COVID heroes at 7pm every night. When hospital shifts were changing, neighbors would hang out of their apartment windows to bang pots and clap for the workers heading home or to work. At a time when anyone without an essential job was forced to quarantine, it was one of the few ways the public could show our appreciation.

Did the nightly ritual really help anyone other than the celebrants? Did the free meals they delivered to the hospitals make the lives of the staff a little more bearable - even though health care workers needed a lengthy decontamination just to grab a slice of pizza? Did these gestures mean anything at all?

It certainly wasn't enough.

What first responders were experiencing, again, is something usually attributed to military veterans: moral injury. Similar to but different from PTSD, it centers on survivor guilt and the feeling that you've failed to prevent something that contradicts your values. People were dying alone and terrified, far away from friends and family. And all the medical staff could do was push aside their own grief and move to the next patient. Amrapali Maitra, an internal medicine doctor in Boston, recognized an unmet need and ran wellness programs for the residents at Brigham and Women's Hospital.

> Phone call after phone call she heard the same message: *We can't take watching these lonely deaths.*[4]

Again, the cracks in the healthcare system were already evident, but they were fully exposed when COVID hit: unprofitable rural hospitals closed, people in those communities hundreds of miles away from trauma centers; staffing decisions were outsourced to bean counters, more concerned with the bottom line than patient care; clinics in minority communities, often the only sources of medical care for people with little or no insurance, were shuttered. And in every part of the country, in big cities and suburbs, small towns and rural communities, in nursing homes and medical centers, front line workers were paying a terrible price.

In a scene from *The First Wave*, medical staff gather for a group session in the hospital to talk about the trauma they're witnessing. But the real toll is the physical, emotional and mental exhaustion. The lack of sleep, missing of regular meals, denying self-care. It's the confusion over protocols, the constant delays and equipment shortages. It's the necessity of drastically curtailing the normal human contact with patients and colleagues that defines their calling. There is no escape. When they finish their marathon shifts, they make their way home, subject to all the quarantine restrictions the rest of us are chafing against. They stay masked up to ride deserted subways or drive home. Normally, their commute would be an opportunity to decompress, to take a mental and physical deep breath and process their day before greeting families. But it's no longer enough.

Like Nora, they come home and repeat a necessary ritual: stand in the hallway to strip off and stuff their work clothes in a garbage bag, and then rush to the bathroom to shower. They may be isolated in a different part of their home, to avoid coming into contact with a roommate or family members. Or they may return home to an empty apartment, switching from a crowded workplace to a silent space. Neighbors might be banging pans to show admiration for their sacrifice, but it doesn't replace a needed hug.

In addition to the first responders working in an institutional setting, EMTs and paramedics were responding to an unprecedented number of calls. Between March 27 and April 7, 2020. New York City's 911 center averaged more than 6,400 calls a day, up from 4,500 before COVID. To put that in perspective, the total on many days was higher than on 9/11. During roughly the same period, the FDNY responded to 2,192 cases of deaths at home (an average of 130 a day), almost 400 percent higher than the same time period in 2019. There were days when more New Yorkers died at home than were confirmed dead from COVID. Why were so many people dying at home, and what was the cause of death?

The city was not counting deaths at home as probable COVID deaths. But then *The Gothamist* ran an April 7, 2020, story on these numbers, In the first few weeks of the pandemic, an average of 245 New Yorkers died from COVID each day; another 200 (up from the pre-pandemic average of 20-25) died at home, many with no definitive cause of death. Admittedly, not all were from COVID. Some were due to heart attacks or other chronic conditions; others involved people too afraid to seek treatment at a time when hospitals were not considered safe. But without a confirmed test result, the medical examiner's office could only flag them as a possible COVID death.

The numbers of home calls alone overwhelmed the resources of paramedics and EMTs multiple times a day. On a normal day, EMTs and paramedics in New York City would respond to 20 calls for cardiac arrest. That number surged as high as 187 calls in one day.

The mental health toll of this pace became apparent early on.

Those EMTs and paramedics are the lowest paid first responders in New York City. Anthony Almojera, a 17-year veteran EMS lieutenant and union leader with FDNY, admitted he'd seen more death in the first year of COVID than in the previous decade. By the time he was interviewed for *The Guardian* article, nearly half the EMTs and paramedics had tested positive for COVID. Five died, but that number does not include those who work for private emergency response companies. All five of the dead were non-white, another example of the racial disparities that COVID laid bare. In that same period, three FDNY EMS workers died by suicide. Almojera knew one of them, 38-year-old Matthew Keene, a nine-year veteran. He last spoke with him a week before his death.

> "You can't say enough nice things about the guy," he said. "I wish he had mentioned even a hint of [his struggles] on the phone. And I would have shared how I was feeling through all this."[5]

The mental health issues for first responders, including risk of suicide, mirror those of military veterans. With both groups we expect total devotion to their jobs because lives are on the line. And though mental health services have grown in recent years for veterans, the medical community has been slow to address a problem that exploded during COVID.

Many state licensing boards require physicians to disclose mental health conditions and treatment, possibly in ways that do not comply with the Americans with Disability Act. The shame and stigma of seeking mental health treatment is part of the medical establishment culture. Even before COVID, over 40 percent of physicians said they'd be reluctant to disclose any mental health treatment (medication or therapy) for fear of losing their accreditation or jobs. That reluctance would prove deadly.

Dr. Lorna Breen,
undated photo, drlornabreen.org

At the beginning of March 2020, Dr. Laura Breen was on a spring break ski trip to Montana with her sister, Jennifer Feist. Breen was the medical director of the emergency department at New York-Presbyterian Allen Hospital, and assistant professor at Columbia University Vagelos College of Physicians and Surgeons. Her residency at Long Island Jewish Medical Center had earned her certification in emergency medicine and internal medicine. She grew up thinking being a doctor in Manhattan would make for a 'cool' life.

She returned to New York from her trip on March 14. Highly organized and deeply invested in emergency medicine, Dr. Breen tackled the beginning days of COVID with her usual focus and passion. But the last week of March, a time when 20 percent of her physician colleagues were in quarantine, she tested positive for the virus. Despite sleeping 16 hours a day, not unusual for COVID patients, she kept in touch with friends, family and colleagues. On April 1, three days after her fever broke, Breen returned to work, at a time when her hospital was treating three times as many patients as usual.

When a friend checked on her a few days later, the stresses were already obvious. Normally someone who slept soundly for eight hours a night, Breen had insomnia. And she began to fear for her job because she was unable to keep up with the unprecedented demands placed on her. She admitted to her sister Jennifer that she wanted to die.

In response, her sister and two friends picked up Breen and drove her to the emergency department at the University of Virginia Medical Center, near Feist's home. She was admitted to their in-patient psychiatric unit, where their mother had worked as a psychiatric nurse for two decades. Breen stayed for eleven days.

But during her stay, while ostensibly healing, Breen still worried about her career. Steps were taken to begin a leave of absence upon her return, but it wasn't enough to ease her mind. Five days after her release to her family, Dr. Laura Breen died by suicide.

As COVID exploded, the prevalence of mental health problems in first responders surged. Was it burnout? That certainly contributed, but it was more than just the toll of long hours with little rest.

We honor veterans with parades. We honor first responders by banging pots and pans. These professions necessarily include constant exposure to life-threatening situations, injury, pain. They should be honored for doing the work most of us would reject. But even without the added element of COVID, the trauma associated with these careers takes a toll. This is one of the reasons why physicians die by suicide at a rate almost double that of the general population.

The stigma of being unable to continue a career that you love had to be addressed. Two years into the pandemic, on March 18, 2022, President Biden signed the Dr. Lorna

Breen Health Care Provider Protection Act to honor the medical emergency professional. This legislation is the first to allocate funding for training health profession students, residents and others in evidence-informed strategies to reduce and prevent the common fall-out: mental health conditions and substance use disorders. Its passage, supported by over 70 health-related organizations such as the American Medical Association and the American College of Emergency Physicians, was spearheaded by the nonprofit Dr. Laura Breen Heroes' Foundation, founded by Dr. Breen's sister and brother-in-law. The foundation works for reform in three areas:

- Advising the healthcare industry to implement well-being initiatives;

- Building awareness of these issues to reduce the stigma;

- Funding research and programs that will reduce health care professional burnout and improve provider well-being.

Dr. Dougé knows the importance of their work. She stepped back from full-time work in October 2021 to attend to her own burnout and mental health and switch to contract work. Now she serves on the foundation's board and speakers bureau, to call attention to the dire strains of her chosen profession.

Because Dr. Breen died at the beginning of the pandemic, when severe restrictions were imposed on groups, her friends and colleagues could not gather to mourn her. There were Zoom memorials, which many felt were inadequate. So at 7pm, when other New Yorkers leaned out of their windows to clap and bang pans, a group of her colleagues would occasionally meet on the corner of 72nd St. and Central Park West, by Strawberry Fields. They would clap, too. As Dr. Bernard Chang explained, it was their only chance to look each other in the eye and say, "Oh, my God, she's gone."

Burying Their Friends

*But what I'm learning lately is
it's a lot harder when the body you're zipping up
is a face you know or a face of someone you love.[1]*

A strange new virus remaining in a body long after death, infecting anyone who comes into contact with it, sounds like a filmmaker's pitch to a Hollywood producer. It also harks back to the early days of the AIDS epidemic, when funeral homes refused to handle the bodies of anyone who died from that disease, and cemeteries refused burial. Everything was new and frightening.

While the studies conducted in 2022 by a Japanese researcher at Chiba University have not yet been published as of this writing, the initial findings are sobering: traces of COVID infection were found in corpses as long as 17 days after death. The risk of transmission is obviously greatest between people who are alive, but it still confirms the fears of last responders.

Last responders? We all know the designation of first responder: emergency department medical staff, EMTs, law enforcement, paramedics, firefighters. The first people on the scene when there's an emergency. But until the third year of COVID, I'd never heard the term 'last responders.' That category includes coroners, medical examiners, funeral workers, morgue attendants, cemetery staff. They're the people who transport bodies, conduct autopsies and embalming, and assist with funeral rituals: the people who ensure that the dead are treated with dignity. Most of us don't think about them until we need their services.

Workers loading bodies into refrigerated trucks,
politico.com, Sept. 22, 2020.

Medical examiners across the country were swamped during COVID. The accrediting body for forensic pathologists recommends conducting no more than 250 autopsies a year. With COVID - along with spikes in the number of deaths due to homicides, overdoses and even car accidents - that number was routinely exceeded by 20%.

"We do more than 250. Most do," said Dr. Gregory Hess, chief medical examiner of Pima County, Arizona, which encompasses Tucson. "I think it's hard for most offices to stick to that guideline nowadays."[2]

As of early 2022, there were about 500 full-time, board-certified forensic pathologists in the US. Medical examiners around the country requested state funding to hire additional pathologists, but some governors cut or eliminated funding increases. The National Association of Medical Examiners currently lists openings for more jobs than the number of newly certified forensic pathologists who graduate each year. Because of these challenges, NAME was forced to relax the limit of 250 autopsies a year, but hopes to keep it under 325.

The vast majority of people who died from COVID died in a hospital, so the cause of death was known. Those who die of known causes are sent to funeral homes. Those who died suddenly, violently, or whose cause of death is undetermined, are sent to a medical examiner for testing or autopsy.

The CDC reported in February 2022, that 914,000 US deaths were clearly attributed to COVID. During the same time period, they saw an additional 113,000 'excess' deaths; in Los Angeles County alone, an increase of nearly 35 percent. Those deaths broke down to 40 percent overdoses, 40 percent natural deaths, 20 percent homicides. A large percentage of those were among the homeless population.

Forensic pathology is challenging work. Though the training is equal to that of a heart surgeon, because they tend to work for government agencies, the pay is about half. Dr. Jeffrey Barnard, chief medical examiner of Dallas County, explained the challenges of recruitment:

Not everyone is cut out of the work, Barnard said. Dealing with homicides, suicides and overdoses is stressful. On top of that is the need to interact with the criminal justice system, which is not the norm for most medical disciplines.

"A lot of times you have to deal with lawyers and judges and then dueling experts," he said. "Not everyone is built to withstand what goes on in the courtroom. A lot of people figure, 'I can sit behind my microscope, make diagnoses, send out my bills and go home versus doing this kind of thing.'"[3]

Sometimes the backlog springs from the matter of issuing death certificates.

One would assume that it would be fairly easy to determine how many people have died from COVID by examining death certificates. But, like many things associated with this pandemic, it's not.

The certificate itself is fairly straightforward, though may vary slightly from state to state. The first part lists the 'immediate cause of death,' followed by any 'conditions that led to the immediate cause.' The second part asks for citing conditions that did not set off the events that led to the death, but still contributed to it. That became the offensive part for many families: their loved one was going to die from cancer anyway. Why list COVID, even if it hastened the death?

The official numbers, then, originate from death certificates. And while we mourn over one million American deaths from COVID, that number is likely underestimated. Remember that we did not have tests early on to determine if a patient had COVID. Many people, turned away from hospitals because they weren't sick enough to be admitted, died at home. Had those people been tested and autopsied, would we have a more accurate count? Of course, but the backlog of bodies to be autopsied and prepared for burial would be even greater. And that additional process piles on additional grief for the friends and family left behind. And for those whose job is to take care of the dead.

Michael Fowler is the coroner of Dougherty County, Georgia. His work has taken him from local floods to twenty-three international disasters to sorting remains at

Ground Zero in New York. He's seen it all. But COVID was different, as he explained in May 2020.

> But what I'm learning lately is, it's a lot harder when the body you're zipping up is a face you know or a face of someone you love. I've lived in this town [Albany, GA] for my whole life. This disaster came to *my* community. At least thirty of these victims are people I knew by name or considered my friends. Six of our preachers in this county have died. I've broken bread with all of those people. I've lost probably seven or eight more I know from church. Two neighbors. Three school friends. The probate judge who had the office next to mine at the courthouse. These are my contemporaries... The sad truth is that I'm almost getting used to it.[4]

Upon a death, family members and others would normally prepare a body for burial as part of religious and cultural traditions. Rituals would usually include washing and dressing the body, or practicing 'angel care,' a Japanese ritual in which orifices are filled with cotton pads. But at the beginning of COVID, many common rituals were prohibited. Bodies of those who died in hospitals were often taken directly to burial sites, like the infamous Hart Island in New York City, bypassing overwhelmed funeral homes. Everyone was flying blind, forced to improvise what measures might need to be taken, even when that felt extreme and disrespectful to the dead. There was, in fact, precedent. The Ebola virus outbreak, which occurred 2014-2016, affected every part of the body, so there was a clear risk to anyone handling those bodies or embalming them. When COVID first hit, it made sense to take that similar position.

But last responders were on the front lines, too, for this pandemic, putting their lives - as well as the lives of their coworkers and families - in danger by just doing their jobs. The risks they faced, especially at the beginning, were clearly defined by Peter Teahen, a funeral home owner in Cedar Rapids, Iowa.

"A few weeks into the pandemic, he was called to the home of someone who had died. After seeing the body, he spoke with the family. 'And only then did anybody tell me that the person who died had COVID, and all the family members in the same house were positive,' he said.

Although unsure of the source, Teahen soon contracted the virus. 'One of the hardest things for me to do was tell my wife I was COVID-positive,' he said, knowing too well what the virus was capable

of. 'I brought it home. I could have killed my wife...
How do you live with something like that?'"5

In normal times, it's not unusual for funeral directors to
handle the arrangements for friends and colleagues. They
still did that during COVID. In Black communities in particular, funeral homes occupy a unique position. They
are as much a focal point of the community as churches.
Baltimore funeral director Hari Close, a member of the
National Funeral Directors and Morticians Association,
saw his numbers jump from around 20 funerals a month
to over 60.

When the pandemic first began, there was little known
about whether the virus was still present and a commu-
nicable danger after a person died. So Close insisted on
doing embalmings himself, to minimize the risk to his
coworkers. Autopsies require using a saw that releases
particles into the air, a risk that he and others in his profession were accustomed to, but which now gave them
pause. Embalming then became optional because so little
was known about the risks. Perhaps for the first time since
the early days of AIDS, funeral workers wondered if what
they were doing could kill them.

To complicate matters, last responders were excluded
from priority distribution of PPE or vaccines, requiring

them to lobby individual governments for these lifesaving factors. Unlike frontline hospital staff, no one offered to collect and distribute the supplies they required to be safe. As citizens were searching the internet and Home Depot for masks for their family, funeral home directors were searching, too, to keep their staff safe.

Hari Close's professional association, with an entirely Black membership, saw a significant number of deaths in their ranks during the pandemic. But COVID was not cited as a cause of death for most of them, because the stigma was so high in the Black community, sadly echoing the same dynamic among Blacks during the early days of AIDS. It was devastating for Close on a personal and professional level, because "you're losing your mentor, you're losing your colleagues that you shared. It shows how vulnerable we are."

Peter Teahen, the funeral director exposed to COVID when he processed a corpse, is no stranger to crises. He has served in leadership roles following such events as the United Airlines crash in Sioux City, Iowa in 1989, the Oklahoma City bombing, 9/11 in New York City, Hurricane Katrina, and the 2010 earthquake in Haiti. But COVID posed a far different challenge than those disasters for him:

"One of the more serious parts of this is the unknown," Teagen says, referring to the still evolving understanding of the virus. "COVID doesn't die with the patient. All the staff dealing with the deceased are just as susceptible to getting COVID as if they were in the hospital environment."[7]

The possibility of contracting this frightening new virus soon became an everyday concern. No matter how careful they were, breakthrough cases – especially in times of limited PPE and no vaccines - were always possible. The fear of transmitting the virus to coworkers and family members raised anxiety.

The mental health impact on last responders is not something most people consider. The numbers of bodies these workers handled quickly soared. But the stresses were not only for their physical well-being.

The commonality in all these workers is the desire to treat the deceased with dignity, and comfort those left behind. It is a calling no less admirable than any other in health care. But in a matter of weeks, COVID changed every aspect of their business. It strained those occupational goals to the breaking point. Bodies were stacked in refrigerated trucks in hospital parking lots because the few funeral homes willing to accept them could not process the backlog quickly.

Funeral directors were forced to drastically limit in-person contact. That meant families and friends could not meet in person to plan the services, choose flowers, schedule viewings, and select photos for newspaper obituaries.

During COVID, wakes and viewings were brief and held only for a few members of immediate families. Funeral services were also limited, including at graveside, with mourners often forced to remain in their cars. Guidance on safety guidelines from the CDC was unclear but seemed to haphazardly settle on a limit of ten people, including the funeral staff. That meant there was no room for friends to attend and say goodbye.

Many funeral homes pivoted to live-streaming services. That at least gave friends and family members the opportunity to come together virtually, especially at a time when travel was discouraged.

But funeral directors and other last responders aren't trained to offer virtual condolences. They live lives of service: direct, in-person, compassionate service. The inability to do their regular work of offering comfort weighed heavily.

When the chaplain at Poteat-Wakefield Funeral Directors in Albany, Georgia, arrived for a funeral service, he was sent directly to the hospital by its proprietor, Jeffrey F. Wakefield, Sr. Not to provide assistance but because he was obviously very ill. There he was diagnosed with COVID and died four days later. "He was a dependable, dedicated employee," Mr. Wakefield said. "To lose him was devastating."

On March 15, 2020, the Centers for Disease Control and Prevention issued guidelines for mass gatherings. At the time, most people believed that COVID would only last a matter of weeks. Therefore, their guidelines recommended that events of 50 or more people be canceled or postponed for eight weeks. But the following week, now operating on the assumption that COVID would only last until the end of the month, the Trump White House issued their own guidelines, advising Americans to avoid social gatherings of more than 10 people until March 31. Of course, that was extended, first through April, then longer. But that didn't mean that every funeral home followed that restrictive policy.

Interpretation of the policies varied, depending on the comfort level of the funeral home operator. Did 'ten people' mean ten total for a visitation or service? Did 'ten people' mean a cap on the viewing room or in the funeral parlor? Did 'ten people' mean ten people at a time but in rotation? The latter meant that the risk of exposure was much greater, involving mourners lined up outside to get into the funeral home. And who was included in the ten? Many funeral homes counted their own employees in that number, which restricted the number of family members. Friends were not included in their calculations. That limit was also enforced at the graveside, which led to thousands of funerals that required mourners to remain in their cars. There were even restrictions on the number of vehicles in a funeral procession. One funeral home offered an ingenious if unconventional solution: a drive-thru open-casket viewing.

Houses of worship were subject to the same restrictions for funerals as regular religious services; even the Supreme Court agreed. But some states designated churches and synagogues exempt from any restrictions. And some churches opted to simply ignore the restrictions in place and pay the fines if caught.

Among the most powerful funeral rituals are those for military and veterans: taps played by a horn, guns salute, ritual flag-folding ceremony, ending with the presentation of the banner to the survivors. Often the attendees include those who served with the deceased, battle buddies gathering together for one last chance to show respect for their fallen comrade. None of that was allowed during COVID. The best that mourners could expect was to watch a silent interment from their cars.

Rituals are important to those who mourn. They're also important to the funeral home operators, who see their calling as one of supporting their communities in difficult times. COVID meant they not only were severely restricted from their duties, but had to keep in constant contact with state, local and federal government agencies to ensure that they were in compliance. Occasionally, funeral home operators decided to go ahead on services without restrictions, which created super-spreader events. That was not good for anyone's business.

These restrictions posed a personal and professional challenge. Funeral homes are not considered cutting-edge when it comes to the ways they conduct the rituals around a death. That shortfall came into sharp focus when COVID restrictions were imposed and people began to demand live-streaming of viewings and services.

Live-streaming an event as important as a funeral isn't just a matter of turning on your phone. It's not free. It requires tech-savvy personnel. It requires security in place so that the live-stream isn't bombed by strangers, something that happened a lot in those early days. People were shocked, then, when YouTube shut down live-streams of funerals because they included copyrighted music, normally not an issue with an in-person service. Copyright restrictions are typically relaxed for religious services, so that had to be resolved.

The advantages of live-streaming are obvious: mourners, especially friends in those early pandemic days when attendance was banned beyond immediate family, were able to gather together, albeit virtually. People who were unable to travel because of the pandemic, or their own health or limited finances, were included. It's not ideal, of course. Nothing virtual can replace the comfort of being with others who mourn, including the ability to hug and laugh and cry together. But these COVID-era restrictions became a newly normalized part of mourning which ultimately benefits friends the most.

Live-streaming, too, gave a small measure of comfort to those last responders, stifled in their ability to honor the dead, especially those they lived and worked with. The service admittedly wasn't ideal, and wasn't what anyone truly wanted. But it was the only way they could serve their communities and keep them safe.

The Show
Must Go On...
Or Not

In the dark times
Will there also be singing?
Yes, in the dark times there will also be singing.
About the dark times.[1]

One of the most famous theater traditions is 'the show must go on.' Last-minute adjustments will be made to ensure the audience sees their regularly-scheduled, high-quality performance. Wardrobes malfunction, sets fall, microphones go dead, performers are injured. Understudies, swings, and even directors go on to replace a sick cast member. An understudy is someone in the cast ensemble who steps in to replace a lead or supporting performer. A swing is a performer not in the regular cast who learns multiple ensemble roles and fills in as needed. Audiences are forgiving, and often love to be able to brag that they were there when an understudy shines and a star is born.

Karin Schall, chalking at Al Hirschfeld Theatre,
New York City, June 13, 2020, with permission.

When various industries shut down at the beginning of COVID, most of them experienced at most weeks or a few months of restricted activity. Restaurants pivoted to take-out and online orders, then to outdoors-only dining. Sporting events were played in empty ballparks and stadiums. Big-box stores and grocery stores held senior hours and prepared orders for pickup in the parking lot. But the arts faced a different set of challenges.

Broadway theater is an integral part of New York City's history and economy. The first theater in the US opened on Broadway in 1735, though it wasn't until the late 1800s that a theater district formed farther uptown. That district - its parameters set between Sixth and Eighth Avenues, 41st to 54th Streets - is currently home to forty-one theaters. They seat between 500 and 1900 people, and before COVID, it wasn't unusual for all forty-one theaters to be booked.

For the 2018-2019 season, the last full season before COVID, the Broadway League reported that the industry contributed $14.7 billion to the New York City economy, supporting 96,900 jobs. No, there were not 96,900 jobs on Broadway. But those productions not only spent money building sets, paying performers, and buying advertising. Their patrons – 65 percent of whom were tourists – also booked flights and hotel rooms, took Ubers and cabs, ate in restaurants, shopped and bought souvenirs. Any disruption in the status quo would have far-reaching effects.

On Sept. 11, 2001, Broadway shut down, like much of the city, in the wake of the terrorist attack on the World

Trade Center. Our collective sense of security was shattered. Then the anthrax scares followed. Out-of-towners couldn't help but wonder if it was safe to go to New York. Is the water safe, the air? Will there be another attack? And as often happens in the immediate aftermath of a crisis, the arts felt unimportant.

The sentiment in Mayor Giuliani's administration was that New York City could be perceived as safe if Broadway was open. The theaters reopened on Sept. 13. Aggressive marketing, including hotel and restaurant discounts, and appeals to local government to save Broadway (while, sadly ignoring off- and off-off-Broadway organizations). The effort resulted in Broadway attendance returning to normal within six months.

Similarly, after Hurricane Sandy hit in 2012, the shows were back up and running in four days. 'The show must go on' still worked.

However, that tradition was sorely tested - and some would say ended - when COVID hit.

One of the universal truths of working in theater is that, with very rare exceptions, you make a fraction of the money you would if you were working on a film. That goes for everyone, not just the performers. Film lives forever;

stage productions exist only in the moment. One might think that its ephemeral quality would make your work more valuable, more lucrative, but it doesn't. Most people consider the arts an avocation, a hobby, something to do until you face reality and get a 'real' job. They don't stop to think about the years of training, the crushing rejections, the constant pressure to improve. Just like those who look at modern art and believe their four-year-old could do the same thing, people feel free to disrespect those in their profession on the stage. Yet within the larger theater community, there is a belief that Broadway is the pinnacle of the performing arts, the goal, achievable only by a small fraction of professional and aspiring artists and technicians.

I happened to be in New York City the second week of March 2020, for what was supposed to be several weeks of book signings and events on the east coast, concluding with the AIDSWatch advocacy conference in Washington, DC. When I left Chicago, though, I wasn't sure how long I'd be gone. Was this coronavirus thing really that serious? Was I at risk?

I had one theater ticket, for Saturday, March 14, at Playwrights Horizon. I was looking forward to seeing *Unknown Soldier*, the final musical composed by Michael Friedman. But on Thursday, March 12, at 5:00pm, the theater world in New York was shut down by order of Gov. Cuomo, as did the Metropolitan Museum of Art and countless other cultural institutions. The only people left working would be box office staff, refunding ticket sales and rescheduling.

That same week, Javier Munoz was a lucky man. The veteran Broadway performer, who starred in both *In the Heights* and *Hamilton*, was in great demand. He was performing a one-man show, *A Sign of the Times*, at Theater 511. On his days off, he flew to Atlanta to play the doctor in the film *Three Months*. He finished shooting in Atlanta and returned to New York on March 9. Life was about to change.

> People on the plane were starting to wipe down things. No masks. I don't understand why I didn't get it. End of February [I was] getting scared - in the theater, airports, planes, etc. Last flight into New York City was March 9. Tuesday I was exhausted and took that day and 11th off. Had an audition on March 12. Starting to discuss anxiety but... it was on my mind. I was trying to finish my work, but didn't feel like it was going to change my life.[2]

On Wednesday, March 11, he wrote to company management.

I just want to go on record, I'm going to do my job, but I don't feel safe and it feels terrifying. This thing is spreading so quickly, I'm going to be in a black box theater, with a live audience unmasked. I'd prefer that we do something about that, but I'll show up.[3]

Despite his concerns, he did not expect what happened next.

I was waiting for the train Thursday morning after the audition to get ready before the show that night, when I got a text from the stage manager saying Broadway League announced it's shutting down. 'Come clear out your dressing room. Go straight to the theater now or it will be closed and you won't be able to get in.' Happened to be staff there to let me in. I packed up all my things. So disorienting, so heartbreaking. I couldn't wrap my brain around what was happening to us. Broadway is shutting down?? I was crying when I was packing up.[4]

He realized later how lucky he was. Many performers did not have the chance to clear out their dressing rooms and wouldn't be able to return for over a year.

His next paycheck, $100 for a Broadway Cares/Equity Fights AIDS virtual event, would arrive in June.

No one knew when Broadway would be back. The initial estimate was that the shutdown would last about two weeks. That proved to be wildly optimistic. Then it was a month, two months, six months.

Other industries and events shut down overnight, including the NCAA basketball tournament at Madison Square Garden, but perhaps none as completely as live theater. Restaurants, stores and even museums eventually reopened with timed entry and reduced capacity. But not Broadway, especially after Governor Cuomo issued a ban on gatherings of more than 500 people. The economics of Broadway - where theater seats routinely sell for hundreds of dollars and eight-figure budgets are not unusual - made limiting audiences to less than 500 people economically impractical. That's one reason why it turned out to be the last major New York City industry to return. The reality was that there would be fifteen months without Broadway performances.

When negotiations began on stimulus packages, some theaters were granted PPP loans to pay their employees. But that was a temporary fix to tide them over during what they assumed would be a brief stoppage. The level of unemployment in the arts - virtually 100 percent - was reminiscent of the Great Depression. But unlike other industries that received generous government funding, like airlines, hospitality, and auto manufacturers, there was no groundswell of support for the arts. There would be no new version of Roosevelt's Works Progress Administration, which hired over 10,000 artists in theater, music, writing and visual art. The output created by the WPA workforce ranged from stage plays and musicals, to traveling art exhibitions, and iconic murals still on display almost a century later in government buildings. But in 2020, if you were in the arts, you could not look to your government to help your industry survive.

Many people who work in theater have other jobs that pay the bills between shows: waiting tables, office temp, teaching. But those jobs weren't available now, because of restrictions on inside dining, events, and office work. While the general public was eager to support restaurants and small businesses, they were restricted to ordering take-out. In addition to inside dining, catered events like weddings, conferences, and fundraising galas, were canceled. That fallback option was gone. Theater people had to take care of their own.

Broadway Cares/Equity Fights AIDS pivoted quickly from spectacular public events like the Easter Bonnet and

Broadway Backwards that raise millions, to virtual appeals. On March 17, 2020, BCEFA created the COVID-19 Emergency Assistance Fund to support programs providing financial support and health care to members of the entertainment industry, including the Entertainment Community Fund (formerly the Actors Fund). They would eventually raise almost $10 million.

Live theater, like education and religious rituals, is a communal experience. Pro-shots, or professionally filmed onstage performances, are great for conveying the look and feel of a play or musical. They cannot, however, replicate the tingle of excitement of sitting in a crowded theater, listening to the overture of your favorite musical as the house lights dim. But theatergoers were desperate to experience live theater in any way they could.

We demanded that Disney+ move up the premiere of *Hamilton* so we could watch it *now*. But what was going on? Why was the Performing Arts Library at Lincoln Center not making their collection of filmed Broadway shows virtually available to everyone? People who worked on Broadway were facing something that no other industry felt: over a year of unemployment, and severe restrictions on maintaining their talents. We demanded that they continue to entertain us, but how? Should they have donated their time to keep us happy? Despite millions of people increasing their streaming subscriptions, should we be expected to pay to watch stage work, though it was on screen and not in person?

Some members of the Broadway community were among the New Yorkers who fled the city in search of safety from the deadly virus. Among them were playwright Terrence McNally and his producer husband, Tom Kirdahy, who drove to Sarasota, where they owned a home. McNally, at 81, was in a risk group for virtually any infection, having lost a lung to cancer and suffering from COPD. But relocating was not enough to save McNally: he became the first recorded coronavirus death in Sarasota County on March 24, 2020, less than two weeks after Broadway shut down. McNally, the recipient of five Tony Awards for plays and musicals, as well as a special Tony Award for lifetime achievement in 2019, became the first prominent name in the New York theater community to die during COVID.

The tributes poured out upon word of his death. But one Broadway mourning tradition, reserved for the titans of the Great White Way, was not available. The ultimate tribute - to honor people who enriched Broadway - is to dim the lights. About 15 minutes before the curtains rise, the marquee lights on all theaters go dark for a minute, to signify the loss of that talent. The tradition started in 1952, when the lights were dimmed for Gertrude Lawrence, who died of cancer three weeks after performing in a matinee of *The King and I.* But it wasn't until 1980 when the practice became tradition. Not every theater is required to dim their lights. But it is a simple, powerful tribute to someone who made a difference in their profession.

Dimming the lights is not exclusively a Broadway tribute. In Chicago, on a cold night in February 2022, the death of influential *Chicago Tribune* and *Chicago Daily News* theater critic Richard Christiansen prompted actors, producers, reporters and other theater professionals to gather at Petterino's restaurants. This critic had helped launch the careers of local theater greats like David Mamet, Gary Sinise, and Amy Morton. After sharing stories and toasts, the mourners walked next door to the Goodman Theater, where the marquee lights were dimmed.

Early on in the pandemic, the inability to continue normal grief rituals was deeply felt. Even outdoor gatherings at a safe distance were few and far between. They didn't feel cathartic enough for people who lost a friend they loved. So the Broadway community did what the rest of us eventually realized was the only effective COVID response: pivot to virtual events.

The first tribute to Terrence McNally took place two weeks after his death: a Zoom reading of his play, *Lips Together,*

Teeth Apart, with Zachary Quinto, Jesse Tyler Ferguson, Celia Keenan-Bolger, and Ari Gaynor. It was a fundraiser for Broadway Cares/Equity Fights AIDS and raised $75,000. In addition, a virtual tribute was held by the Drama League Awards, and a 2018 documentary about McNally, *Every Act of Life,* was rerun on PBS. These events had to be sufficient in the short-term for the friends who were mourning. The community finally came together for a traditional memorial service on November 1, 2021, nineteen months after McNally's death.

That celebration of McNally's life, held at the Gerald Schoenfeld Theater, was free and open to the public. The friends who eulogized him, including those handpicked by him to speak before his death, reflected on their shared work experiences, as well as the off-stage friendships that developed from those shows. Actor Nathan Lane, a friend and collaborator for over thirty years, hailed the professional legacy McNally left, but also his personal legacy as a friend who was generous to a fault.

There were many other losses in the theater community, people who might not be household names or worth a mention on the nightly news. But they were people whose lives were devoted to bringing truth and joy to their performances.

One of the musicals shut down by COVID was *Waitress,* which opened in 2016. Based on the 2007 film, the show follows baker and waitress Jenna, who is in an abusive marriage. After unexpectedly becoming pregnant, she begins an affair with her doctor. She ultimately enters a pie-making contest, seeing its grand prize as her way out of all her troubles. The charming and boyishly handsome Nick Cordero played Jenna's oppressive husband, Earl.

When *Waitress* shut down, Cordero and his wife, Amanda Kloots, decided to leave the city with their infant son for Los Angeles, in search of work and safety.

Like many, Cordero became sick quickly. Because of COVID restrictions at the hospital, Kloots's ability to see him in person was severely curtailed. Sympathetic nurses held up his phone so she could Facetime with him. She kept theater community friends, colleagues and a growing number of fans updated on Cordero's battle with COVID via social media. Even people who never knew Cordero became caught up in this real-life drama. Unfortunately, the situation quickly escalated. Because of blood clots, Cordero's leg had to be amputated. And he lay in a coma for weeks. Kloots bravely chronicled it all and drew the admiration and support of hundreds of thousands across the world.

Nick Cordero, once a physically fit song-and-dance man in perfect health, died July 5, 2020. He was only 41. His death flew in the face of conventional wisdom at the time: that only people who were old or had significant comorbidities could die from COVID.

How could Cordero's *Waitress* family, the people he worked with onstage and backstage nightly, honor him? They were now scattered around the country, unable to gather together to mourn. But they found a way to mourn en masse when the show reopened in September, 2021, a limited run cut even shorter because of a spike in COVID cases.

At the theater's concession stand, audience members could purchase Cordero's CD and his wife's memoir about her marriage and her husband's fight to stay alive. In addition, the company of *Waitress* paid tribute to Cordero in two other meaningful ways. First, in the *Playbill* was this simple tribute:

> Our *Waitress* family and the entire Broadway community lost a bright light in 2020. We dedicate these performances to the memory of Nick Cordero, who will be deeply missed but never forgotten.[5]

Drew Gehling, who returned to the cast when *Waitress* reopened, explained the second way the theater family honored Cordero's memory:

> 'The hardest part of coming back was the first day of rehearsal. Chris Fitzgerald, Eric Anderson and I all looked at each other and couldn't help but feel like something was missing,' he said. 'But then we quickly realized that he's with us every day. He was such an integral part of the creation of the piece. We've named a pie after him in the show and have actually permanently altered a set piece of the diner in the show, in every company, all over the world to include a big old slice of 'Live Your Life' pie. It's become a huge part of the heart of what the show is.' The new pie name refers to Cordero's hit song, which people worldwide played from their homes daily during his battle with COVID-19.[6]

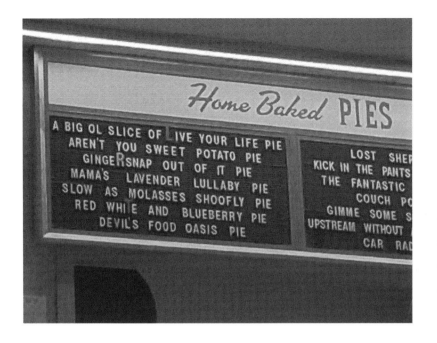

Author photo of pie board on the set of Waitress,
Barrymore Theatre, New York City, Oct. 5, 2021.

Eleanor Vassili of *NPR* interviewed two performers from
Phantom of the Opera the day their show reopened, Oct. 22,
2021. Kelly Jeanne Grant and Janet Saia talked to Story-
Corps about someone who was missing: costume dresser,
Jennifer Arnold, who died from COVID in March 2020.

> Grant: When things go wrong backstage, she al-
> ways had a real sense of irony and spunk and spice,
> and she would always make you see the funny even
> when you felt like it was falling apart.

Jen was famous for these matchboxes that she made.

Saia: She would give them as gifts for people.

Grant: When Jen passed...we organized this online memorial. And it was huge, from cast and crew members to the carpenters and everyone strangely had chosen to bring her matchboxes with the personalized little details that she had given to each one of us.

Saia: We lit candles.

Grant: And at some point, someone said, now everybody turn off your lights for her.

Saia: You know, she loved being a part of the theater world. So I think lighting her matches and remembering her brings her back to the theater, where she loved to be.[7]

One of Janet Saia's matchboxes,
a gift from Jennifer Arnold, Storycorp

Not every casualty on Broadway during COVID died from the virus. In September 2019, acclaimed Broadway actor and singer Rebecca Luker performed in concert with fellow soprano, Sally Wilfert. While her voice was as powerful and angelic as always, she realized she was experiencing mysterious physical challenges. The two women were planning to go into the studio in March 2020, to record an album, "All The Girls" but COVID canceled that plan. Luker's final public concert that month, and a virtual one in June, were a struggle for her. By the time it was safe to go into a studio again, in August, Luker could no longer sing. She'd been diagnosed with amyotrophic lateral sclerosis (ALS) or Lou Gehrig's Disease.

Luker had previously triumphed in major classic musical theater roles: Maria in *The Sound of Music*, Marian in *The Music Man*, Laurey in *Oklahoma!* But her friends loved her for much more. They loved her fierceness, her sense of humor, her devotion to her husband, fellow Broadway actor Danny Burstein.

That proposed album eventually was produced, though not in a studio. Music director Joseph Thalken and producer Bart Migal mixed new orchestrations around good quality recordings from that prior September concert. The CD was released May 4, 2021 - but this was four months after Luker succumbed to ALS. A tribute, indeed, but how could her friends properly mark her tragic passing?

The same day as the CD release, Luker's friends hosted a virtual concert, *Becca*, to benefit Target ALS, with all ticket sales through the Rebecca Luker Memorial Fund benefiting ALS research. They joined together to reminisce, to laugh, to cry, to tell stories and to sing. Among them were Great White Way heavyweights Kristin Chenoweth,

Norm Lewis, Michael Cerveris - and dear friend and fellow soprano Sally Wilfert.

The annual Tony Awards telecast, like other awards shows, honors prominent people in the industry who died the previous year. The list for their 2021 In Memoriam contained 264 names of theater notables who died between June 8, 2020 and September 26, 2021. If the lights on Broadway were dimmed for one person every night, six nights a week, it would take ten months to honor them all.

In May 2021, New York State Governor Andrew Cuomo declared that Broadway was finally open for business. His announcement took everyone by surprise, including the New York theater community. Broadway shows that had been shut down for over a year can't just open overnight. The industry struggled to catch up with his proclamation. When Broadway reopened in September 2021, there were several days of panels and performances in Times Square to officially celebrate the comeback. But the industry did not heal immediately. After all, COVID was still claiming tens of thousands of lives.

Karin Schall, chalking in Shubert Alley, New York City,
July 30, 2021, with permission.

Strict theater guidelines, set by the city and the unions, required performers to be vaccinated. Audience members had to show proof of vaccination and wear masks (properly, or the ushers would yell at you) the whole time they were inside the theater. Every production employed COVID 'enforcers' to ensure that they were in compliance and that everyone onstage and off was safe. But because no one lives in a bubble, there were breakthrough cases during this time. It had taken fifteen months to get back to regular performances. No production could afford multiple performance cancellations. So understudies and swings became the new heroes.

Throughout the fall of 2021, they were called upon to replace cast members on a regular basis, usually with only a few hours' notice. And while that's basically the definition of their jobs, for maybe the first time in their careers, they were truly seen and appreciated. After all, they were the reason performances were not canceled. Still, it was an unsettling way of life on Broadway for the first few months back.

So much disruption, so much loss. Even with Broadway back, it's far from normal, which mirrors the experience of other industries. COVID changed everything and everyone, as *Hamilton* actor Javier Munoz, living with HIV himself, admitted:

> I learned my community is in a lot of pain, experiencing more challenges than I was ever privy to. Stories I had no idea about. I'd like to think I'm walking away with a greater sense of gentleness towards others and myself. I'm not always the best at taking care of my health. The ways I treat myself need to be kind and gentle; just do better. Extend

that to everyone I work with and come in contact with. Don't tolerate a lot of ignorance, for Trump or anyone who supports him. The grace I want to extend is within reason, but...

I'm changed from my experience. I feel greatly changed.[8]

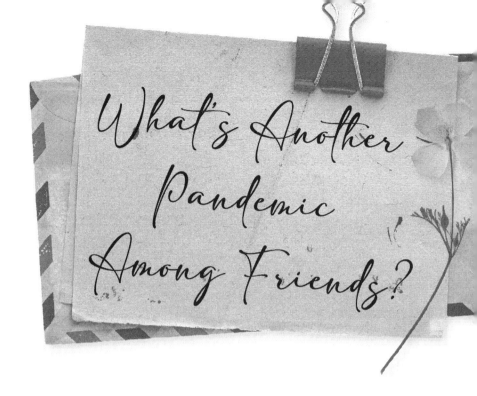

What's Another Pandemic Among Friends?

Dear gawd, not again![1]

Very early in the pandemic, I began to experience emotional reactions that confused me. I first attributed the confusion to a general state of shock over the swift series of events that shut down our lives. But they persisted for a couple weeks until I finally recognized what was going on: déjà vu.

I wrote a blog post on April 1, 2020, two weeks after returning to Chicago from my drastically shortened east coast trip. It took that long for some clarity:

I'm not sure what the first trigger was. It might have been a picture like this one, medical personnel dressed in 'space suits' to remain safe from their patients.

It might have been the word 'pandemic'.

It might have been 'only certain people will get this virus, not me'.

It might have been stories of meal deliveries left on porches, or recommendations that counters and doorknobs be wiped down with disinfectants.

It might have been a Republican president indifferent at best to the suffering of those whose lives he did not consider important.

It might have been the blame, the pointing fingers, the demonizing.

It might have been the insistence of many people to carry on their lives as usual, no matter what the consequences of their actions.

At the beginning of March, I thought I was the only person who felt a persistent, nagging sense of déjà vu. The beginning of the AIDS epidemic was almost 40 years ago. The coronavirus pandemic is not the same (a frequent topic of heated discussions on Facebook). But there are enough similarities that those of us who remember those dark days are now experiencing waves of grief and yes, anger.

"Do you think that your experiences in the AIDS community are affecting how you feel now?" my therapist asked last week. My first reaction was "Well, duh." But since then, that question has been guiding me, for better or worse.

One of the lingering behaviors from that period of time is that if I don't hear from a friend for a while, I assume something terrible has happened to them. Maybe not dead, but something really bad. It certainly comes from that time when people often disappeared, their names surfacing only when you saw their obituary in the weekly LGBT paper. People died quickly then. The speed at which they died was stunning, though they were lucky. Others lingered for months, in and out of hospitals where they were treated like lepers, sometimes dying alone.

Last week I started contacting all the friends I hadn't heard from lately. A series of emails, texts, phone calls, Facebook messages assured me that all were alive and mostly well. Many of them have conditions that put them at risk if they contract the coronavirus. The friends in New York worried me the most, but I was relieved to hear back from all but one. That one I'm still worried about.

I told my therapist that I expect that someone I know will die from this virus, maybe more than one someone. It might be one of those people who's already at risk. It might be someone who was otherwise healthy. That kind of surprise is what I fear the most.

It's easy to be on edge these days. Our world is full of unknowns, even more so than usual. Our routines have been upended; our finances shaky at best. We all know people who have lost their jobs, maybe their businesses, too.

The whole world is grieving for the losses that mount each day along with the bodies. And as much as we try to pull together - and we have - it would be a mistake to ignore the sense of loss we feel.

My therapist asked what I do when I'm triggered, now an everyday occurrence. I told her that I stop what I'm doing when I have these moments, these flashbacks. For too many years, I pushed those thoughts aside, buried them deep inside me so that when they finally came out, I was overwhelmed. Now I acknowledge them and take a moment to remember that terrible time when my friends were dying and damn few people cared. And then I shift gears. I do something else, go for a walk, do the laundry, post links to resources that my friends can use: anything that feels productive. The moment passes, but it's not ignored, because I learned the hard way that ignoring isn't healthy.

I see a lot of my friends, long term survivors in the AIDS community, who are similarly triggered. They were the ones I reached out to first. I can't tell them how to deal with this because we all face grief and trauma in our way. But I hope they know I understand, that I'm willing to listen and help in whatever way I can.

When this is all over - and it will be someday - we will gather again to hug and kiss and dance. We'll marvel at how we survived not one but two pandemics. And then we'll dance some more.[2]

The hugging and kissing and dancing part took longer than I expected, but then no one knew how long COVID would upend our lives. Looking back, my first blog posts on the subject before this one were painfully optimistic; it was clear I was desperate for some sliver of hope to hang onto. But by that April, our resolve to get through this temporary glitch in our lives was already beginning to weaken. The two-week order to shut down had already been extended, and it seemed likely it could be extended again. How long could this go on?

For more than forty years, if you ask long-term survivors in the HIV/AIDS community, because that's how long it's gone on for them. It's no wonder they felt triggered during COVID.

> I don't know about you, but when I first heard the news of the COVID-19 pandemic, my first response was, *Dear gawd, not again!* And sure enough, the first year and a half of the COVID pandemic closely mirrored our experience of the HIV/AIDS pandemic. The triggers were plenty and went off constantly. The lack of knowledge about this "new" virus mirrored our confusion about what was causing AIDS. The stupid rumors about COVID promulgated by bigoted know-nothings mirrored the hurtful, unscientific bigoted rumors that spread about HIV and

AIDS. The animus and violence directed towards our Asian friends during COVID mirrored memories of how gay men and drug users and sex workers were demonized and violently attacked because of AIDS. Our government's incredibly slow and stupid response to the COVID pandemic mirrored our government's slow and stupid response to the HIV pandemic. The constantly growing death toll from COVID triggered memories of picking up the B.A.R. [Bay Area Reporter] on Thursday mornings and immediately turning to the obituary pages to see who had died that week. And finally, sheltering-in-place and quarantining pushed many of us back into the kind of isolation and loneliness we had just begun to conquer. We've had one hell of an ugly ride since early 2020.[3]

When COVID first struck, it didn't take long for vulnerable populations to be identified: people over 60, anyone with comorbidities, anyone immunocompromised. For the first time in decades, I again feared for the lives of my friends with HIV or AIDS.

It was not unreasonable to worry about people who were unlucky enough to fit all three of those demographics. Even those who were virally suppressed were often over 60 and harbored other health concerns.

By the summer of 2020, seven friends with HIV or AIDS had contracted COVID. None were hospitalized for COVID, but for weeks I held my breath. It wasn't until the end of the year that my fears were calmed by an interview with Gregg Gonsalves, an HIV-positive ACT UP veteran who is an Associate Professor of Epidemiology (Microbial Division) at Yale School of Public Health and Associate (Adjunct) Professor of Law at Yale Law School.

"...if you're suppressed in antiretroviral therapy, you should be treated as any other patient coming into a hospital. You shouldn't be considered at higher risk than probably people of your own age group. People living with HIV have an uncontrolled virus and have frank immunosuppression. I think that's another story, but if you're controlled on antiretro-viral therapy, nobody's suggesting that you should have a different outcome with COVID than your HIV negative peers."[4]

What this pointed out, though, is that the determining factor was whether you were virally suppressed through antiretroviral therapy. That's a big 'if.' This is where HIV and COVID were most similar: we could see clearly the racial and economic disparities.

"All the social determinants and social inequities that are generating HIV infections, the same inequities are also generating COVID infections."[5]

In other words, if you were lucky enough to be in treatment for HIV, then able to adhere to that treatment with no debilitating side effects, and finally able to afford that treatment, you were okay. If not, you weren't.

Long-term survivors were now watching the same disparities with COVID. And sometimes the triggers were eerily specific.

"I've really been irritated with all the so-called surprise around the racial disparities," says Tony Christon-Walker, director of prevention and community partnerships for AIDS Alabama. "This is not new."[6]

Just like the early days of AIDS, in the early days of COVID it was not unheard of for people with the virus to be kicked out of their homes. Sometimes it was their landlord, sometimes roommates or even family members who were afraid of being infected. These suddenly homeless people wound up on the streets or in their cars. Shelters struggled to develop policies, especially for congregate settings where dozens of single people (the 40 percent of the homeless not seeking shelter with family members) were forced into a shared facility. Ongoing safety issues aside, spreading COVID was a certainty. And that was assuming the shelter would admit them at all.

New York City has a right-to-shelter law on the books, which entitles requests for housing to be honored, even if that person is sick. But what to do with people forced out of their homes because they're contagious? Many, both families and singles, were sent to quarantine elsewhere, in some of the 83 percent of the city's hotel rooms that were vacant by early April. This process owes much to the hard work of HIV/AIDS activists over the years. In 1985, New York City formed the HIV/AIDS Services Administration (HASA) to help people with HIV/AIDS to access emergency financial and housing services. Thus the achievements from one pandemic created an effective framework for facing another one.

The coronavirus and HIV pandemics are not interchangeable. There are similarities but they are not the same. But researchers had the benefit of years of trial and error to develop HIV/AIDS treatments that formed the beginning of their work to vaccinate the world against the coronavirus.

For the HIV community, HAART is a regimen that changed everything for people with the disease. The combination of drugs – known as the 'cocktail' – resulted in a literal 'Lazarus Effect,' where patients on death's doorstep rebounded to a near-normal existence. People who never expected to live to age 30 were now members of AARP and drawing Social Security. And now they were wondering if after they survived one pandemic, they would succumb to a second one.

> When I feel emotionally triggered by the old feelings of dread and despair, I try and remember: now is not then. This is not that virus.[7]

Like military vets triggered by suppressed grief and survivor guilt, AIDS-era survivors had a lot to unpack, mentally and emotionally. Were they going to lose friends... again? HIV-positive people who'd lost scores of friends and lovers from AIDS now feared a repeat with COVID.

Dr. Lawrence Mass is a New York-based physician and writer, who co-founded GMHC (Gay Men's Health Crisis) in 1982 with Larry Kramer, Paul Popham, Nathan Fain, Paul Rapoport, and Edmund White. It continues as the oldest and largest HIV/AIDS service organization in the country. Mass and Kramer's friendship began over a decade before HIV became known. His response to the beginning of COVID - when the HIV/AIDS epidemic still had not ended - was typical of many in that community.

To say that there was a sense of deja vu would be an understatement. The biggest difference between early public responses to COVID versus those of AIDS is that the public awareness of COVID was initially strong, however spectacularly ignorant, bellicose, political (as opposed to scientific) and incompetent its presidential leadership. This was in contrast to the early period of AIDS, when leadership of any kind, even bad leadership, was invisible because it was nonexistent. From the beginning, and precisely as with AIDS, we had jackasses and liars - Trump cynically seizing the spotlight to promote himself and his politics, having learned nothing from the lessons of Reagan, who remained silent and did nothing at all.[8]

Organizations and programs tasked to serve the unique needs of long-term survivors now had to face the challenge of helping them navigate COVID in a way that most people did not. This anxiety necessitated a new kind of grief support.

Long-term survivor support groups, a lifeline for many, could not meet in person. The San Francisco-based Honoring Our Experience pivoted to virtual writing groups; they still meet weekly. While not ideal, the benefit of virtual gatherings was that people scattered across the country, including areas where there was little if any support for long-term survivors, could bond with others experiencing the same emotions.

New online working groups formed to share accurate, up-to-date information on COVID as it affected those with HIV/AIDS, whether or not they were on antiretroviral drugs.

The writing and art projects encouraged long-term survivors to look at COVID through the lens of AIDS. What feelings were being triggered? Had they lost a sense of community by being unable to meet in person? Did they mostly feel despair, or did they believe that surviving HIV/AIDS gave them a resilience that would get them through COVID? How could they use their past experience to make things better for their friends?

In the summer of 2020, I asked several of the long-term survivors in my last book, *Fag Hags, Divas and Moms: The Legacy of Straight Women in the AIDS Community*, to share their thoughts on my blog. All straight women, they'd survived through accidents of luck, through decades of advocacy, through the kindness of friends. One who shared her concerns was Rosa E. Martinez-Colón, longtime activist and educator in Chicago.

I fear for my loved ones. My friend who is HIV positive and is still working. She has not disclosed her status to her employer because she fears she may lose her job. Day in and day out she goes to work and prays that she is not exposed to Covid-19.

Back in the 90s, in the midst of the HIV/AIDS pandemic, I never hesitated to hug my friends and loved ones. Every Saturday in our support groups, I loved welcoming them and hugged and kissed them, anticipating an evening where we would cry hard but also laugh just as hard. Today, it has been 48 days since I last hugged someone. And I miss that. I can't wait to be able to do it again; to be able to see family and friends and embrace them in a tight hug and kiss them and tell them how much I love them. For now, I have to make do with Zoom, WhatsApp or FaceTime video calls. I have to send virtual hugs and kisses. But there will be a time when we will be able to do that in person again.[9]

Rosa E. Martinez-Colón, undated photo,
reprinted with permission.

From Nancy Duncan, veteran ACT UP and Planned Par-
enthood activist on Long Island:

> My immune system is stable, but I do fear getting
> this just like most people. I'm trying my best to be
> as safe as I can be, but I thought I was being safe
> in 1985 when I contracted HIV...I fought so hard to
> stay alive back then and now I feel like I'm fight-
> ing again against an invisible enemy trying to
> kill everyone.[10]

Long-term survivors used that hard-earned strength and experience during COVID to consciously create safe, reliable places, even online. That's what Princess Dallas Lyle did, with an online HIV support group meeting.

> Service work has changed for me as a result of the COVID pandemic. It has been back to basics for me. I have learned how to be a better listener and help people on their journey toward feeling whole and loved. I was hosting a Zoom social hour when a man who was terminally ill entered the virtual gathering from his hospital bed. He shared that he was dying alone, and we were there for him. We all cried, and I told him we loved him and played music he enjoyed. That experience was a gift, to be there for him at his time of need. It's realities like this that keep me serving. If I can make a difference in just one person's life, I have fulfilled my destiny. I will always hold onto that hope.[11]

These examples are not to imply that long-term survivors did all of their work online. Many took to the streets again to march for the dead and fight for the living. They joined forces with established groups like ACT UP, Rise and Resist, Right 2 Health, and Black Lives Matter, because they understood the critical importance of coalitions. They survived HIV/AIDS because of direct action and were energized once again during COVID by political engagement.

When right-wing evangelist Franklin Graham's Samaritan Purse organization set up an emergency field hospital in Central Park, activists called out his chronic discrimination towards the LGBTQ community. When they saw the life-threatening effects of community health center closings, they demanded that services continue. They demonstrated against an indifferent government and greedy pharmaceutical companies. Their experience made them effective activists once more.

HIV/AIDS long-term survivors have much to teach us about navigating a second pandemic. And it's fortunate that many of them, newly re-energized, have been willing to share their hard-won experience to lead and inspire the next generation.

*****

Larry Kramer, a co-founder of GMHC and the inspiration for ACT UP (AIDS Coalition to Unleash Power), died May 27, 2020. The cause of his death was pneumonia. The news was not entirely unexpected, since he had been in ill health for years. But it was still shocking, as his passing felt like the ultimate connection between the two epidemics of HIV and COVID.

Sometimes described as 'the angriest man in the world,' for his decades of activism, Kramer was also a prolific writer and playwright. At the time of his death, he was working on a play, *An Army of Lovers Must Not Die*, about gay men living through three crises: HIV/AIDS, COVID, and the physical deterioration of their bodies. Joined with his groundbreaking 1985 play *The Normal Heart*, written in the dark days of AIDS, *An Army of Lovers* could have been a poignant bookend for the long-term survivor community.

Kramer believed his anger was justified to fight rampant indifference, especially in a world that considered gay men's lives of no value. For him, the AIDS protest slogan 'Silence Equals Death' was the absolute truth. Members of his own community, even close friends, did not escape his wrath. Kramer felt justified confronting long-time friends like Larry Mass, who was on the same side of the barricades.

> We will not see Larry's likes again, though this isn't an argument that Larry himself sanctioned. One of the main reasons he was so angry with us all is that he couldn't see why we weren't all doing what he

was doing, and just as angrily, loudly, passionately and effectively.

When someone like me would point out that we weren't all Larry Kramers, that not everyone has the capacity to be a leader of such strength and influence, Larry would have none of it. He once confronted me: Why wasn't I ANGRIER!?! He wasn't having any of my excuses or rationalizations, including the fact that I was a person in recovery who had to learn the hard way - that is, very personally - to be wary of anger, justified or not.[12]

Long-time HIV/AIDS activist Peter Staley reminded us of this dynamic in his Facebook post the day Kramer's death was announced:

I just got off the phone with Tony Fauci. I broke the news to him via text earlier today. We're both surprised how hard this is hitting. We both cried on the call.

I've told Larry to fuck-off so many times over the last thirty years that I didn't expect to break down sobbing when he died. His husband David kept the recent hospitalization under wraps, not wanting to deal with a million phone calls. I found out only last week, and only after Larry was doing much better. As of Saturday, he was still improving. I only heard this morning that everything spiraled in the last 48 hours.

Larry's timing couldn't be worse. The community he loved can't come together -- as only we can -- in a jam-packed room, to remember him. We can't cry as one and hear our community's most soaring words, with arms draped on shoulders in loving support. Broadway has no lights to dim, which it surely would have.

Can we please do this next year?

Fuck, this hurts. I keep flashing back to those early ACT UP meetings. I put on a good show, always in mission-mode. But the more I've written about those years, the more I've remembered how scared I was -- diagnosed when I was 24 years old. It was all bottled up, but I was terrified. Those meetings gave me the only hope I could find back then. Larry orchestrated the launch of ACT UP. He plotted with Eric Sawyer and others, planting calls for a new group during the Q&A after his speech.

Larry Kramer founded a movement, and I'm alive because of that. Millions more can say the same. All his faults fade away in the wake of our thanks.[13]

Dr. Anthony Fauci of the National Institutes of Health was not only someone from Kramer's past; he was part of his present, too. When COVID shut down the country just two months before his death, Kramer reached out to his former nemesis, who he once described as 'an incompetent idiot.' Over many years, they'd declared a truce of sorts and learned to work together on their shared goal of ending HIV/AIDS. Kramer expressed concern for Fauci's new role as the public health face of COVID. Here they were, two long-time HIV/AIDS warriors, now facing a second, eerily similar virus that targeted vulnerable populations. The fact that Fauci was again working under a Republican president who preferred to ignore the epidemic was certainly not lost on either man.

Larry Kramer, undated photo, actupny.com

"Indeed, politics did step in the way of science back in the 1980s, but it was a different kind of politics," Fauci observed. "There wasn't necessarily the divisiveness that we see now in our political landscape today. Back then, the federal government, particularly the first term of the Reagan administration, didn't recognize or even pay attention to the importance of the emerging AIDS outbreak. There was a lot of stigma, because the disease mostly and severely affected the gay population during an administration that was very conservative. At that time, the gay community was not readily accepted as an important political group, as they are now, and thank God that's changed dramatically over the years."

And over the last few months, plenty has been written about masks being the new condoms in terms of helping protect against contracting a virus; however, the battle raging between mask wearers and those who won't because of their civil liberties isn't the first time that a fight broke out about wearing protection.[14]

In an episode of the progressive radio show *Democracy Now* , host Amy Goodman asked Gregg Gonsalves about those parallels:

Amy Goodman: The comparison of the plague of AIDS and the plague of COVID19?

Gregg Gonsalves: Well, we have two presidents who have botched the response to two different epidemics. Larry said, I think on a CBS piece in the '80s, that we died from AIDS because we were disposable people. We didn't matter. Well, there's a new era and new epidemic and a new set of disposable people, whether they're dying in nursing homes, or they're dying in communities of color, in meatpacking plants, in prisons. For those of us who are in ACT UP, we recognize what's going on now, and it's been beyond benign neglect. It's malevolence. It's premeditated murder. And Larry knew very well what was happening then, and he knew what was happening now in the epidemic that we're facing today."[15]

Six weeks before his death, Kramer was interviewed by Michael Shnayerson for *Vanity Fair*. At the end of his interview with the 84-year-old writer and activist, Shnayerson asked if the fact that these two pandemics, HIV and COVID, occurred one after the other held any special significance.

"Kramer was quiet for a moment; I heard him breathing on the line. It was a stupid question, I was about to tell him. These were viruses; they didn't mean anything.

'That evil exists in the world,' he managed at last."[16]

How Do We Remember the Dead?

We have no visual signs of grieving but we need it.
We need it more than ever... If I can change one thing
right now, I'd create that.[1]

Throughout history, people have asked this question: How do we properly memorialize the departed? We hold rituals immediately following someone's death; there is the ceremonial washing of the body, then religious services, and a journey to the final resting place for interment. Those are all important and relevant to honoring each individual's death. We've already seen numerous heartfelt and ingenious ways that people in all walks of life found to honor their friends who died during COVID. These memorials were intensely personal, even under the limitations of the pandemic.

But how do we remember large numbers of people? Specifically, thousands of people who died on the same day or under similar circumstances?

During the inauguration of President Joe Biden in January 2021, among the many dignified events was a lighting ceremony held at the Lincoln Memorial Reflecting Pool to mourn COVID casualties. Four hundred lights were installed, each representing 1,000 dead (the total at the time). It was a powerful reminder of the enormity of the loss, which would eventually more than double. There was an added historical significance to that site, as noted by history professor and author Micki McElya, in an interview with Mary Louise Kelly on *NPR*, the day before the inauguration.

> Sharing grief brings people together, especially in the United States, like nothing else. This is a vast country of an enormous and varied population... Yet it's in moments of national mourning, it's in moments of collective grief and collective honor that we come together, that we experience those bonds of nationhood and community across all of

these many different lines of difference. Often lines of difference that, of course, we understand all too well are fraught and violent and difficult. And there can be no unity, there can be no collectivity without a shared sense of belonging, without a shared sense of community in this nation. And that's what collective grief offers.[2]

The iconography of national memorials to war dead changed dramatically with Maya Lin's 1982 design of the Vietnam Memorial in Washington, DC. Until then, war memorials were grandiose and representational, soaring monuments to the honored dead: among the imagery was officers on horseback, soldiers raising flags, majestic eagles. Lin was an undergraduate at Yale when her design was announced after a national competition.

Outrage to her winning design was swift. It didn't look like other memorials. It looked like a black, v-shaped slash in the ground, not a traditional depiction of the brave dead. She was young - 21 - and a woman. Her Chinese heritage unleashed a torrent of anti-Asian bigotry. But her design included something that few large memorials included: tens of thousands of names. The names of every American serviceman or woman who died was engraved in chronological order. Several hundred names have been added since it was dedicated, bringing the current total to 58,318.

If you walk around many cities and towns, you will notice memorial plaques on the walls of post offices, train stations, schools, parks, even department stores, all listing the employees or alumni who died in one of the world wars. They appear as a few dozen names in alphabetical order: simple, direct, respectful. So the memorial listing of names of the war dead began long before Lin's design. She envisioned her memorial as a symbol of the pain caused by war and its casualties. "I imagined taking a knife and cutting into the earth, opening it up, and with the passage of time, that initial violence and pain would heal," why does this end like this?

When the families of the thousands of victims of the 9/11 attack on the World Trade Center insisted that all the names be listed in any memorial on the site, they were considering a smaller number than what is listed on the Wall. The total eventually grew to 2,977, which included all those who died on that site, at the Pentagon and in Shanksville, Pennsylvania, as well as the six people who died in the 1993 World Trade Center bombing. Because the date itself was not a factor, they fought for 'relational' listing of the names: people were grouped alongside co-workers or fellow passengers.

Those are permanent exhibits in a fixed spot. You must go to Washington or New York to view them in person, though there are smaller traveling versions of the Vietnam Wall.

The NAMES Project AIDS Memorial Quilt began in 1987 to remember those who died from AIDS. Each panel is the size of a burial plot, handmade by the loved ones of the deceased. Eight panels are sewn together into a section. There are almost 50,000 panels in tribute to 110,000 people, and the Quilt is still growing. New panels are constantly being added. But at 54 tons and 1.2 million square feet, it is too large to display in its entirety anymore. Sections can be requested for display around the country. For Pride Month 2022, 3,000 panels were displayed in Golden Gate Park in San Francisco, the largest display in over a decade.

2,977

58,318

110,000

That's a lot of names to display, honoring the dead. But how do you even begin to consider creating a physical memorial to over a million people who have died from COVID, just in the United States alone? The numbers, after all, are still growing for a pandemic that took more lives by the end of April 2020 than fatal casualties in the entire 21-year Vietnam War. The question of the look of the COVID memorial has been debated almost from the outset of the pandemic.

It must be noted that all three of those memorials provide a contemplative physical space to grieve, whether permanent or temporary. They also often exist in lieu of individual burial plots. The remains of only 1,647 people who died on 9/11 have been identified and returned to the families for burial. Many of those memorialized on the AIDS Quilt were shunned by their families, leaving friends or strangers to handle burial or cremation details. But because these were tragedies that were experienced by the entire country, a central location to honor those lost also serves as an opportunity to bring people together.

They all have websites where you can search for names and view an individual's engraving or panel. But is that an emotionally satisfying alternative? Just as gathering together for wakes and funerals enables people to collectively grieve, don't we need physical memorials, too?

Maya Lin's design for the Vietnam Memorial in Washington, DC, is considered an 'open' memorial.

"Open memorials respond to the unfinished work of grief and the lack of historic closure. And now, a new generation of them responds also to the unfinished work of mass death. Where there's no agreement on basic facts - whether the war in Vietnam was just or whether wearing a face mask is necessary - only an open memorial makes sense."[3]

Lin's masterwork was not satisfying to many traditionalists who wanted representational art to commemorate the Vietnam casualties. Two years later, a traditional sculpture, Frederick Hart's bronze "Three Soldiers," was added near the Wall, and later, another statue commemorating servicewomen. Finally, a plaque honoring those who died later as a result of their service was also added. It's worth debating whether those additions deepened the experience of the initial memorial.

If you need a more common example of an open memorial, look no further than the items left on the spot where someone died violently: ghost bikes, flowers, teddy bears, crosses, and devotional candles. They spring up without warning, spontaneous outpourings of community grief that are soon swept away by municipal cleaning workers.

There have been many open memorials during COVID. The wrought-iron fence at Green-Wood Cemetery in

Brooklyn was covered with tributes to those who died of COVID, people who were denied normal funeral rituals. The drawings and photographs were evocative of the desperate displays after 9/11, on fences near the ruins of the World Trade Center, from friends and families searching for the missing. Those photos became an unintentional yet temporary memorial.

There have been a number of physical memorials to honor those who have died from COVID, but they have two things in common. First, they are very restricted in scope. They honor first responders at a hospital, or residents of a particular neighborhood. In April 2021, the state of Ohio dedicated fifteen trees as the COVID-19 Pandemic Memorial Grove in Great Seal State Park in Chillicothe. It honors those who died, those who cared for them, and the sacrifices made.

Second, most of these memorials have been temporary. I visited one in New York City in November 2021. The exhibit of The Hero Art Project offered rotating projections of first responders in the windows of the New York Life Insurance Company across from Madison Square Park. Two months later, it was gone.

Author photo of a panel from The Hero Art Project,
New York Life Insurance Company,
New York City, Oct. 1, 2021

At the Brooklyn Museum in 2022, "A Crack in the Hour-glass" filled a gallery. It was begun in 2020 by artist Rafael Lozano-Hemmer, who described his interactive project as an 'anti-monument.' Participants submitted, via his website, photographs of people who died from COVID. He and his assistants built a sand plotter with a robotic arm and AI imaging processor.

Visitors could watch the plotter create images as the sand streamed down, like an hourglass. When it was finished, the sand was dispersed and recycled, reflecting the transiency of most memorials. The gallery walls were covered with printed images of the sand portraits.

The largest example of a temporary physical memorial to those who died from COVID was Suzanne Brennan Firstenberg's "In America: Remember," an art installation that eventually grew to over 700,000 white flags on the National Mall.

Firstenberg is a visual artist based in Bethesda, MD, who was a hospice volunteer for 25 years. In March 2020, she heard Texas Lt. Gov. Dan Patrick suggest that older Americans should be willing to sacrifice their lives to the coronavirus for the sake of the economy. "That was the straw," she said, when we met at her studio in Bethesda. She was determined to find a way to physically manifest the horror that was happening, to prove that every single life has value.

She decided on the use of flags in her art installation, but what color? Red or blue seemed to provoke politics, and other colors had no special significance to the moment. Firstenberg finally chose white, the color of life and innocence, because no one chose to die from COVID. But

white was also a symbol of surrender, Firstenberg imply-
ing that we gave into this plague and let it happen.

Air Photos Live, In America: How Could This Happen...,
flags display in front of RFK Stadium, permission of
Suzanne Brennan Firstenberg.

The first installation was in the fall of 2020, a display in
front of RFK Stadium that grew to 267,000 over the two
weeks of the exhibit. She assumed it would be a remembrance of what happened and ended, because within a
few months, everything would be back to normal. In fact,
she walked around the installation, insisting to visitors
that "This is not really a memorial."

Her belief that the daily rise in the death toll was temporary echoed a comment by Cleve Jones, founder of the NAMES Project AIDS Memorial Quilt. For its 25th anniversary in 2012, the Quilt returned to the National Mall, though not in its entirety. Its size prohibited that. In a *Smithsonian Magazine* interview that summer, Jones described the power of displaying the Quilt as bearing "witness...it's imperative that we stand on our National Mall and tell people that this is about them. It's about all of us."

By the summer of 2021, Firstenberg realized that because the coronavirus was still raging, and that an exhibit to its casualties would indeed be a memorial. That second display a year after the first one was more than double in size.

Bruce Guthrie, In America: Remember,
National Mall, Washington, DC, 2021

When someone approached the installation on the north side of the Washington Monument, they were greeted by a tally board that displayed the current total of Americans who had died from COVID. Every morning, the number was updated. Workers added more sections and more flags every day. Unlike other permanent and temporary memorials, it was not a static exhibit. It began with 620,000 flags and grew by about 2,000 every day -- just like a cemetery adds gravestones. About 20,000 of those flags had names added by family members..

"People don't really have a good concept of numbers," Firstenberg observed. One can state that 700,000 people died of COVID but visualizing that number of people is almost impossible. She had to find a way to convey the immensity of the nation's loss.

Each one of the 143 sections was 60 ft. x 60 ft. To put that in perspective, all the dead from 9/11 would have only filled about two-thirds of one section. There were a few benches installed for visitors to rest and reflect, but most people wandered around silently or sat on the ground near the flag of someone they lost. The public was invited to submit names, dates and messages that were inscribed by volunteers. Visitors could also dedicate flags and add them to the display.

Despite the polarization of positions regarding COVID, Firstenbeg said there were only a handful of people who objected to the display for political reasons. No damage or destruction was reported, though she did request an increase of security when Jan. 6 insurrectionists were on trial in the capitol.

Politics factored into this second installation in one way. Near the tally board were two signs: one recorded the COVID death toll in New Zealand, a country which enacted severe quarantine measures from the beginning to minimize their casualties. That number signified true leadership to Firstenberg. The other sign showed what the US death toll would have been had the same measures been taken. The sea of white flags, to her, was proof of a lack of leadership.

Taha Clayton, COVID Memorial, Transit Workers Union Local 100, Brooklyn, NY, permission of TWU.

Transit Workers Union Local 100, representing New York City's MTA bus and subway employees, dedicated a permanent COVID memorial in the lobby of their offices in September of 2021. Deemed 'essential' workers, but not prioritized for PPE, the 110 members memorialized (as of press time) serve as a reminder of the cost of going to work during a pandemic. Transit workers were often forgotten as the world ground to a halt, forcing most people to quarantine at home. But first responders and others still needed transportation. The buses and subways kept running, putting operators at risk. How to honor their dead? Union leadership decided on a permanent memorial plaque in their Brooklyn headquarters.

Displayed alongside the plaque is a painting by Brooklyn artist Taha Clayton. It features five union members in the uniforms or attire worn by workers in the seven departments: Maintenance of Way; the Manhattan & Bronx Surface Transit Operating Authority; Car Equipment; Stations; Rapid Transit Operations; MTA Bus/School Bus/Private Operations; and TA Surface. The concept of a central grouping of transit workers demonstrating both grief and strength originated with union staff and leadership in conjunction with the artist. It was fully developed by Taha through a series of sketches that led to the final oil-on-canvas creation.

As powerful as physical memorials may be, it's impossible in this age to imagine any memorial without an online component. Virtual memorials play into the need for accessibility. They allow people all around the country, and the world, to pay their respects. They allow people physically limited or otherwise unable to travel the opportunity to experience the memorial. There have been many online memorials honoring people who died from COVID, as well as Facebook groups.

Is it enough?

Would designating the first Monday of March each year, the accepted beginning of the pandemic, as "COVID Victims Memorial Day" be enough of a memorial?

Of course, none of these COVID-related memorials take into account the 'excess' deaths': the people who died during COVID from other causes. Nor do they include the people whose cause of death was unknown, in the early days before effective testing. Where does that leave the opportunity to grieve for those other people?

The "In Memoriam" tribute is a powerful and accepted segment of any TV awards show. It honors those from that profession - film, theater, music, sports - who died the previous year. But critics usually protest what they see as the unforgivable exclusion of certain people from these memorial rituals. How would a National COVID Memorial, virtual or physical, ensure accuracy, especially considering the fact that not all COVID deaths were accurately recorded?

There is little strong opposition to the concept of a National COVID Memorial, but volatile politics inevitably enter the conversation. Activists from several groups led by Kristin Urquiza, who founded Marked by COVID, managed to get a resolution introduced in the House to designate the first Monday in March as 'COVID-10 Victims and Survivors Memorial Day' before they arrived to meet with members of Congress. Over four dozen activists gathered over Zoom to plan their strategy. You would think this would not be a hard sell. In theory it's a good idea, though it's not a popular topic as we do our best to move on from the most deadly period of the pandemic. The activists were frustrated when some politicians at Congressional meetings tried to frame the request in terms of politics. Their request for a COVID Memorial Day has not been adopted.

If we do build a national memorial, where should it be built: in Washington, DC, to represent the losses of an entire nation? In New York City, where the virus exploded into our national consciousness? Should it - could it - list names engraved in stone for all to see and remember? And the most important question: do we really want or need a physical memorial to the tragedy of COVID?

Some people believe it's premature; after all, COVID hasn't ended. The 9/11 Memorial in New York City took ten years of highly-charged negotiations; the museum took longer. Some believe the enormity of this pandemic renders a proper memorial impractical, if not impossible. And still others believe it's an unhealthy fixation on the past. When I posed the question to Suzanne Brennan Firstenberg, she agreed on the need for a COVID memorial, but with one very significant caveat:

If we're going to have a memorial, it has to include the answers to how did this happen. A memorial without learning doesn't set us up for success next time.[4]

"Your best friend in the whole world"

Will it ever get better?
I have no reasons to tell you it's going to get better.
I have no charts or diagrams. I have no prophecies to share.
But I know this. The more faith we have in the future,
the better we are. And better is
where we want to be. [1]

Music has long been considered a universal language. During COVID, finding comfort and inspiration was a challenge at times, so we turned to music that connected us. Radio was our link to the outside world when we were growing up. The people on the radio became part of our lives, too. We recognized their voices and listened eagerly for any tidbit of information about our favorite singers and musicians. Sometimes we saw them in person at station-sponsored events.

Starting in 1960, progressive rock WXRT 93.1FM in Chicago was known as "Chicago's Finest Rock" station. After a buyout in 2017, changing to adult album alternative, the slogan changed to "Chicago's Home for Music Lovers." But one of the constants has been Terri Hemmert.

Terri Hemmert is one of the most beloved radio personalities in Chicago, and for good reason. Her Sunday morning "Breakfast with the Beatles" draws listeners from around the country on Audacy. Since the late 1970s she has taught a class on the music's origins and development at Columbia College. But her knowledge of music reaches far beyond rock & roll. Her Facebook posts are as likely to describe jazz or folk music or even classical because of her involvement with the Chicago Symphony Orchestra's Classical Encounters series. In addition, she is always willing to support community causes, anything from food drives to AIDS service organizations. And her well-known devotion to the Beatles has found her serving as MC for the annual Fest for Beatles Fans since 1979. She's generous and approachable, with an infectious joy for life.

Terri lost multiple friends during COVID. She devoted Facebook posts to the passing of friends like John Farneda, Sister Jackie, The Rev, and musician John Prine.

> "God does have a wicked sense of humor. So I think God is probably a big fan of John Prine. That's why he called John home way too soon. He just couldn't wait. Who could blame him? He's only human..."[2]

But one casualty in the pandemic stood above all the rest: her fellow DJ at WXRT, Lin Brehmer. Lin and Terri were not just colleagues. They were close friends outside of work. Their mutual admiration society was clear from on-air banter and social media posts.

I think it's safe to say that many of us who listened to WXRT over the years never met Brehmer. Or perhaps we were at many of the same events with him - Cubs home games, concerts at the Metro, fundraisers - without realizing it. He did not stand out in the crowd for exceptional looks or a unique fashion sense. He was an everyman, a large part of his widespread appeal.

*Lin Brehmer and Terri Hemmert, originally posted
Sept. 2, 2016, reprinted with permission of
Cathleen Falsani/Falsani.com*

Brehmer seemed to be everywhere, interested in everything, and always willing to support an important cause.
He loved the Chicago Cubs, and broadcast opening day
for thirty years. He loved the theater community, stadium concerts and intimate clubs. Brehmer was someone
whose tangential but powerful existence enriched ours.

In July of 2022, Lin announced that he was taking a
leave of absence from his WXRT radio show. His long
battle against prostate cancer, though caught early, had

ultimately spread to places "one would rather it did not spread."

"He'll be fine" was the most common response I saw on Facebook. Brehmer simply needed to concentrate on his health for a while and then he'd be back...right? And just to comfort us, he returned to the air for several weeks in November and December.

Terri Hemmert announced Brehmer's death on-air, January 22, 2023. Reactions poured in immediately: from Congressman Mike Quigley, (IL-05) who offered a tribute to his long-time friend on the floor of the House of Representatives, from Brehmer's beloved Chicago Cubs, who paid tribute to him on the Wrigley Field marquee, from rival radio stations and musicians like the band Los Lobos. The majority of tributes came from his listeners.

Now the question remained: how best to honor someone during a pandemic, someone who brought us so much joy? How do you mourn someone you only knew as a voice in the ether?

You turn on your radio.

At a time when we mourned the loss of in-person funerals and memorial services, thousands of people found solace in gathering around their radio to mourn Lin Brehmer. All that day and the next, in tributes led by Terri Hemmert, the people behind the microphones at WXRT remembered their colleague.

It was months before people could gather together to remember Brehmer, fittingly at Yak-Zies, the bar near Wrigley Field where he broadcast live on Cubs home openers. But it was before that, in February, when Hemmert gave her longest, most personal remembrance of her friend.

Ash Wednesday fell a month after the DJ's death. On Facebook that day, in a post that began with childhood memories of gorging on chocolate on Fat Tuesday because that's what you were giving up the next day for Lent, Terri Hemmert segued into her own tribute to Lin Brehmer, beginning with a sentiment he often shared with listeners: Take nothing for granted. It's great to be alive.

> We all take it for granted sometimes. We're human. I'm Catholic. Lin Brehmer went to the church of the air guitar. Atheist. And we totally got each other...Just because we didn't share our concept on why we're here. But we did, though. We both broke bread with friends and reached out to those who don't feel they belong...If it wasn't so patronizing, I'd say he was one of the best Christians I'd ever

met. But that misses the point. It's about love...I miss him. I know you do, too. Boy, do I ever...When he was here he reminded us daily not to take this life for granted. And as long as we think of him, and share stories about him, he's still reminding us. As friends we had a lot in common. And where we didn't, we both loved each other and respected our differences. In this insane time, that's not only necessary, but it may be the thing that saves us. It all goes back to love...What matters is how you're going to live and love with however much time you and I have. And when we return to dust, the stories and laughter and good examples will be as essential as the love from those who have passed, who we've loved...that love is what lives on."[3]

Wrigley Field marquee, Jan. 22, 2023, courtesy of Marquee Sports Network.

*****

There are many reasons why you felt the need to read this book. You were mourning the COVID death of a loved one. You sought further consolation. You needed closure, in whatever way that makes sense to you. You may have been angry that the people around you didn't understand how deeply the death(s) affected you. They may have treated your loss as less. Less important, less life-changing, less valid than the grief experienced by people whose parents or grandparents or partners died. You may have initially agreed with them and believed that, too.

If you did, I hope this book has changed your mind. You're still grieving your friend(s), right? That hasn't changed, no matter how other people view your experience. But I hope you now feel other things, too:

> That you have been forced to do something you may have never imagined doing: saying a final goodbye to a friend who changed your life. Maybe more than one.

That you have permission to grieve your friend in your own way, in your own time.

That your grief is not only valid and important, but life-changing, often in surprising ways.

That your friend occupied a unique role in your life, one that cannot be filled by a hobby or a volunteer shift or the presence of any other person.

That the anger and frustration you feel is both understandable and normal. The pandemic denied you the opportunity to visit with them while they were still alive or honor them in the company of other mourners after they died. Don't minimize your loss by comparing your experience to others.

Know that you are not alone in struggling to find ways to grieve and honor your friend.

Know that no one is strong enough to grieve alone, so now is a good time to stop trying.

Know that you have a right to challenge anyone who tries to minimize or denigrate your grief, because your friendship and loss both deserve respect.

Know that you've learned ways to grieve and honor friends that may inspire you to do something similar. Or completely different.

Know that laughter always has a role in grieving your friend, because it was part of your friendship.

Know that your friendships define you and shape your ability to love all kinds of people who are part of your life.

Know that surviving a worldwide pandemic is no small feat.

Know that you may now feel that your friendships mean more to you now than they did before COVID.

Feel more certain that your understanding of grief and friendship has been clarified by a worldwide pandemic.

I'm not saying you will feel all these things just from reading this book, but I expect you will feel some of them as they relate to your experience and grieving process.

It's too easy in an unrelenting tragedy to react rashly, to stop feeling, especially when you lose more than one friend in a short period of time. Depending on the situation, it may be necessary to shut down your emotions in order to do your job; maybe even for your own survival. But at some point, that ability to compartmentalize will crumble, and grief will make itself known -- whether you want it to or not.

How do you prepare for that?

You wisely surround yourself with uncompromising friends, like the people in this book did. If you now identify with any of those major emotional breakthrough changes in yourself, it means the people you've read about have helped facilitate that realization. They've shared their grief so that you can find your own inspiration and solace and solidarity.

The nature of friendships dramatically changed during COVID. I know mine did. Some withered because of neglect. Some perished due to extreme political differences. Others faded because of a realization that some friendships, no matter how long, were just not healthy.

Conversely, other friendships became strengthened during COVID. Because of a deeper appreciation for each other. Because we both acknowledged that strong friendships require deliberate, regular tending. Because we realized in an era of omnipresent death, when a friend can suddenly disappear forever, there should be no more taking friendships for granted.

Will those good intentions created during the worst of COVID survive beyond the pandemic? Will we go back to taking friendships for granted, even while feeling nostalgic for the days when we finally came together after so much time when COVID kept us forcibly apart? Being human, and given our collective track records on New Year's resolutions, that backsliding in friendships is possible; maybe even likely. But I believe that in the wake of COVID that we'll try harder as people this time, harder than we've ever tried before. We will strive to keep those friendships alive and thriving and central to our lives.

As friends, we may not share DNA. But we do share bad jokes, great taste in music, questionable romantic choices, sometimes dangerous adventures, all-nighters, respect, laughter, tears and love. Friends are the whipped cream on your hot chocolate, the butter on your popcorn. Some are with us for decades, others for months or even weeks. But they all became part of our lives. Like that moment in *The Wizard of Oz* when Dorothy walks outside after the tornado drops her in Munchkinland, friends turn our sometimes dreary sepia-toned lives to glorious Technicolor.

So I hope that when you close this book about death and grieving, you'll do something exquisitely life-affirming: You will pick up the phone and call one of your friends. Tell them, at the risk of profound embarrassment, that you love them. It doesn't have to be a long-winded explanation of all the reasons why you do, nor a Shakespearean declaration, nor a premature eulogy. Just those three little words - I love you - will be enough to express what you know to be true. (Pro tip: if you're not used to doing it, the first time is the hardest. It gets easier.)

If we've learned anything during COVID, it's that we rarely know when we're going to have a last conversation with someone. The universe does not warn us in advance. Therefore, we should not put off a meaningful conversation until it's too late.

Your friends may think you're simply being ridiculous by your declaration; they may be shocked into an uncharacteristic silence. But whether they respond in kind or not, you've done something supremely important.

You've confirmed their importance in your life.

You've assured them that you love them.

And those are two things that every friend deserves to know.

Acknowledgements

The danger of trying to thank everyone who helped bring this book to life is that I might forget someone. Writing a book only looks like a solo endeavor. In reality, it takes a village to help conceptualize, research, write, produce, market, etc. If you've made an important contribution and your name is not here, mea culpa. I can only blame my second concussion and long-COVID. It does not indicate a lack of appreciation of your support. My thanks go to:

My team, led by my magician of an editor, Jay Blotcher, who always knows how to take a sad song and make it better; 100Covers.com who not only designed the cover but formatted the interior and produced social media graphics; Orna Ross at Alliance of Independent Authors, who helped me clearly focus on the potential of all my work.

My beta readers - Gregory Chatman, Jeannine Forrest, Lynn McSorley, Annie Mitchell Smith, Roberta Steele, Carol Greco - whose encouragement and suggestions were welcome at a time when I could no longer be objective about what I wrote.

My Indiegogo supporters - a group of incredibly generous and patient people believed this book was needed, and that I could write it. At a time when COVID was still raging, their support made all the difference. They understood all too well the challenges of grieving friends during a pandemic, as Krishna Stone so simply and eloquently wrote:

I will miss the remarkable DJ Warren Gluck who died on April 29, 2020.

I loved him so much.

For many years, I wrote grant applications for a variety of nonprofit organizations: AIDS, arts, social service. Applying for grants as an individual is a whole different animal. My gratitude to the Illinois Arts Council Agency for seeing value in this project.

A few short months after I began work on this book, I sustained a second concussion. Luckily, I already had a terrific neurologist to turn to right away, Dr. Elliot Roth from the Shirley Ryan Ability Lab. Finding him several years after my first concussion saved my sanity, and possibly my life. Without him, I certainly would not be writing anything more complicated than a grocery list. His guidance made all the difference after my concussions, and again, when I began having issues post-COVID in the fall of 2022. Without his support and patience, along with his team, especially Megan Miedema, you would not be reading this today. I owe him more than he'll ever know.

It took a while for me to fully commit to this book. One day, my therapist, Ashley Wilkins, asked me why. I told her I knew how this kind of writing and research could affect me, and I did not want to go there again. "Were you in therapy then?" "No." "Well, you are now." I owe her a lot, too.

This is my eighth book, but the first one where I had trouble finding people to be interviewed. It was frustrating, but understandable, because their grief was so fresh. Still, I'm amazed, even now, that anyone is willing to open up to me. Some of the people in this book are friends; others were strangers when I approached them. But all of them trusted me with their stories, and I hope they're pleased with the final result.

There are others who helped in ways that may have seemed small, but made a great difference to me, including Gregg Cassin, Krishna Stone, Jim Eigo, Jamie Leo. I also include the women in my Women Nonfiction Authors group, especially because we lost one member in 2022. A few people prefer to remain anonymous, but their support is no less appreciated.

The Chicago Public Library (Edgebrook branch) saved me hundreds of dollars on books I needed for research, and Shakespeare & Co. bookstore in New York cheerfully separated a sizable chunk of money from my wallet.

Because of COVID, I did most of my writing at home, which was not the case on my earlier books. But there were a few semi-regular haunts that stimulated my brain and sometimes provided tea and treats to keep me going: Barnes & Noble Cafe, Drama Book Shop, New York Public Library, Chicago Public Library, Metropolis Coffee House, Nordstrom Cafe.

As with my last book, Facebook provided a surprising number of contacts and a wealth of information, particularly daily recaps from historian Heather Cox Richardson, which popped up with remarkable timing in Facebook Memories.

A special mention to my Nerinx Hall Class of 1970 classmates, especially Lynn McSorley, who held me up when I needed it the most.

Martie McNabb, whose presence in my life has gained importance over time, in ways I could not have predicted: including giving me a book title. Her generosity in including me in her presentations through Let's Reimagine and the Global Grief Conference is deeply appreciated.

My husband, John Chikow and daughter, Emma Noe Chikow. Their support, especially these past three years, means the world to me.

The woman who thought I should write in the first place, Delle Chatman, must be acknowledged. I had no idea on that spring day in 2006, that her unconditional encouragement of my absurd idea - to write a book about people grieving their friends - would change my life. Unlike her, I'd never written a book before, which she did not consider a liability. This is my eighth book, the seventh specifically on that topic (though the other one touches it, too). It's safe to say I could never have predicted that what seemed like a ridiculous idea would change my life. But I believe she knew. And though she died six months after that conversation, she's been with me every step of the way.

And for obvious reasons, I acknowledge you, reading this right now. It means you made your way through stories of grief and resilience in a worldwide pandemic, stories of the power of friendship to shape our lives. Sharing those stories was the real purpose of this book.

My thanks to you all.

Notes

1. Alok Vaid-Menon, "friendship is romance", alokvmenon,com, Feb. 14, 2017, with permission of author.

Eulogy for a Friend

1. Christine Adams, inscription in author's 1970 Nerinx Hall yearbook.

2. Victoria Noe, eulogy for Christy Adams, Feb. 24, 2022.

3. Laura Stanfill, "Breathing Lilacs", from *Alone Together: Love, Grief, and Comfort in the Time of COVID-19*, edited by Jennifer Haupt, Central Avenue Publishing, September 2020, with permission of author.

Friendship in a Pandemic

1. Mahatma Gandhi quote

2. Dr. Joy Miller, "Virtual Grieving: When Pandemic Death Stares Us in the Face", *Forbes*, July 13, 2020, reprinted with permission.

3. Kat Vellos, *We Should Get Together: The Secret to Cultivating Better Friendships*, permission of Kat Vellos, Connection Coach, speaker, and author.

4. Kat Vellos.

5. Dr. Joy Miller.

6. Debra Kamin, "Have You Sent Your Holiday Cards yet?" NY Times Dec. 2, 2020.

7. "A Shared Devotion" NY Times, April 18, 2021.

8. Anonymous writers, Facebook posts, 2023.

9. Mary Schmich, "When it's all over: a pandemic fantasy" *Chicago Tribune* April 10, 2020. Published with permission.

On Sundays, A Clergy Collar and a Hazmat Suit

1. Mary Ann Coyle, SL, "Reflections from the House of Loretto", Aug. 26, 1998, permission of Loretto community

2. Roxane B. Salonen, "North Dakota priest faced multiple crises in 2020, but he's beginning the new year with a hopeful outlook", *Bemidji Pioneer,* Jan. 8, 2021

3. "Voices", KUOW Puget Sound Public Radio, May 6, 2020, with permission

4. "Voices".

5. Tish Harrison Warren, "Why Pastors Are Burning Out", *New York Times*, Aug. 28, 2022.

6. Tish Harrison Warren.

7. Carol Zinn, "LCWR's focus on grief helps sisters find solidarity amid loss of lives, ministries", *Global Sisters Report*, Aug. 14, 2020.

8. Carol Zinn.

9. Carol Zinn.

10. Carol Zinn.

11. Carol Zinn.

12. Sr. Jan Hayes, personal interview, June 22, 2022.

13. Sr. Helen Santamaria, personal interview, Dec. 13, 2022.

14. Charles King, personal interview, Brooklyn, NY, Oct. 14, 2021.

"This is What it Must be Like in a War Zone"

1. Anonymous, interview in New York City, Oct., 2021

2. Emma Goldberg, *Life on the Line: Young Doctors Come of Age in a Pandemic*, quote

3. Dr. Thomas Fisher, *The Emergency: A Year of Healing and Heartbreak in a Chicago ER*, Penguin Random House, 2022, with permission.

4. Emma Goldberg.

5. Martha Pskowski, "'It Doesn't Feel Worth It': Covid is Pushing New York's EMTs to the Brink", *The Guardian*, Feb. 24, 2021.

Burying Their Friends

1. Eli Zaslow, *Voices from the Pandemic,* Doubleday, a division of Penguin Random House LLC, New York, 2021.

2. Michael Allove, "Too Many Bodies, Too Few Forensic Pathologists", *Louisiana Illuminator*, Feb. 25, 2022.

3. Michael Allove.

4. Eli Zaslow.

5. Debra Venzke, "Shining a light on last responders", public-health.uiowa.edu, Jan. 14, 2021.

6. Debra Venzke

The Show Must Go On…Or Not

1. Bertolt Brecht, "Svenburg Poems", *The Collected Poems of Bertolt Brecht*, David Constantine and Tom Kuhn, translators, W. W. Norton, 2019.

2. Javier Munoz personal interview, New York City, Feb. 2, 2022

3. Javier Munoz.

4. Javier Munoz.

5. Broadway.com quote

6. Storycorp quote

7. Javier Munoz.

What's Another Pandemic Among Friends?

1. Hank Trout, remarks at unveiling of David Faulk mural celebrating long-term survivors at Open House, San Francisco, Dec. 20, 2022.

2. "My Second Pandemic", author blog post, victoria-noe.com, April 1, 2020.

3. Hank Trout.

4. "United States of Anxiety - ACT UP Fight COVID", WNYC, Dec. 7, 2020.

5. Jose de Marco, "We have to change the rules: What AIDS activists can teach us about the COVID pandemic", *In These Times*, 8/12/2021.

6. Tim Murphy, "Surprised by the coronavirus racial disparities? These longtime Black HIV providers and activists aren't", thebody.com, April 13, 2020.

7. Bruce Ward, "Not Our First Pandemic: The View from a Long-Term HIV Survivor", *Talkspace newsletter*, June 23, 2020.

8. Larry Mass, personal interview via email, Nov. 3, 2021.

9. Rosa E. Martinez-Colon, "Reflections on COVID-19", blog post, victorianoe.com, May 8, 2020.

10. Nancy Duncan, "Reflections on COVID-19", blog post, victorianoe.com, May 1, 2020.

11. Princess Dallas Lyle, "Giving Back", *Positively Aware*, Jan./Feb. 2023, reprinted with permission.

12. Larry Mass.

13. Peter Staley, Facebook post, May 27, 2020, shared with permission.

14. John Casey, "Dr. Fauci on Larry Kramer, Reagan, and Pandemic Parallels", theadvocate.com, July 24, 2020

15. "Fight Back!" ACT UP Members and Tony Kushner Remember Trail-Blazing Activist Larry Kramer," *Democracy Now!*, May 28, 2020

16. "In One of His Final Interviews Larry Kramer, 83, and Infirm, Still Roared", *Vanity Fair*, 5/28/2020)

How Do We Remember The Dead?

1. Suzanne Brennan Firstenberg, personal interview, Bethesda, MD, Jan. 24, 2022

2. NPR quote

3. Phillip Kennicott, *Washington Post*, April 9, 2021 - TITLE

4. Suzanne Brennan Firstenberg.

"Your Best Friend in the Whole World"

1. Lin Brehmer, Facebook post, Oct. 18, 2022.

2. Terri Hemmert, Facebook post, May 23, 2021, reprinted with permission

3. Terri Hemmert, Facebook post, Feb. 23, 2023, reprinted with permission.

About the Author

Deep into her fourth career, St. Louis native Victoria Noe is a Chicago-based award-winning author, speaker and activist with two degrees in theater. Her *Friend Grief* series - the result of a promise she made to a dying friend - recognizes the importance of friendships in shaping our lives and honors an often disrespected type of grief. Noe's long-time HIV/AIDS activism then led her to write *F*g Hags, Divas and Moms: The Legacy of Straight Women in the AIDS Community*, the groundbreaking book that recognizes the women who changed the course of the epidemic. An accomplished public speaker, she has presented to a wide variety of organizations and events, including ACT UP/London, Mt. Sinai Hospital, the Muse and the Marketplace, BookExpo America, and Open Hand/San Francisco, as well as libraries and bookstores around New York state and the Midwest. During COVID, she led workshops for Let's Reimagine and Global Grief Network, and led writing groups online for Honoring Our Experience. Noe is a member of the Alliance of Independent Authors,

Chicago Writers Association and Nonfiction Authors Association. Her newest book, *What Our Friends Left Behind: Grief and Laughter in a Pandemic,* shares the challenges faced by people who grieved a friend during COVID.

When she's not writing, you can find her online debating politics, the minutiae of musical theater, classic rock, and her St. Louis Cardinals, not necessarily in that order. Try to keep up with her at victorianoe.com and on social media:

Facebook: VictoriaNoeAuthor

Instagram: VictoriaNoe1131

YouTube: @VictoriaNoe

LinkedIn: victorianoeauthor

Books by Victoria Noe

What Our Friends Left Behind:
Grief and Laughter in a Pandemic

F*g Hags, Divas and Moms:
The Legacy of Straight Women in the AIDS Community

Friend Grief and Men: Defying Stereotypes

Friend Grief in the Workplace: More Than an Empty Cubicle

Friend Grief and the Military: Band of Friends

Friend Grief and 9/11: The Forgotten Mourners

Friend Grief and AIDS: Thirty Years of Burying Our Friends

Friend Grief and Anger:
When Your Friend Dies and No One Gives a Damn

Online reviews are always welcome!